White-Collar Unionism in Britain

WHITE-COLLAR UNIONISM IN BRITAIN

A Survey of the Present Position

ROGER LUMLEY

METHUEN & CO LTD
11 New Fetter Lane, London EC4

First published 1973 by
Methuen & Co Ltd

© *1973 Roger Lumley*

Printed in Great Britain by
Ebenezer Baylis and Son Ltd
The Trinity Press, Worcester, and London

SBN 416 24140 9 hardback

SBN 416 24150 6 paperback

Distributed in the U.S.A. by
HARPER & ROW PUBLISHERS, INC.
BARNES & NOBLE IMPORT DIVISION

Contents

Preface

This book is an attempt to pull together some threads in answer to the question 'What is known about white-collar unionism in Britain?'. It aims to consolidate present knowledge in the field, point to areas needing further investigation, and provide a basis for making predictions of likely developments.

Acknowledgements are due to Dr N. H. Cuthbert, Dr H. S. Gill, and Professor R. K. Kelsall, who read various drafts of the work and made useful suggestions.

Finally thanks go to my wife, Carol, for suffering with me.

London
February 1972   Roger Lumley

List of Abbreviations

ABS	Association of Broadcasting Staff
ABT	Association of Building Technicians
ACTSS	Association of Clerical, Technical and Supervisory Staff
ACTT	The Association of Cinematograph, Television and Allied Technicians
AGSRO	Association of Government Supervisors and Radio Officers
ALGES	Association of Local Government Engineers and Surveyors
AMA	Assistant Masters' Association
APECCS	Association of Professional, Executive, Clerical and Computer Staff (Formerly CAWU – Clerical and Administrative Workers' Union)
APOE	Association of Post Office Executives
AScW	See ASTMS
ASSET	See ASTMS
ASTMS	Association of Scientific, Technical and Managerial Staffs (Formerly ASSET – Association of Supervisory Staffs, Executives and Technicians; and AScW – Association of Scientific Workers)
ATTI	Association of Teachers in Technical Institutions
AUEW	Amalgamated Union of Engineering Workers
BAC	British Association of Chemists
BACM	British Association of Colliery Management
BALPA	British Air Line Pilots' Association
BDA	British Dental Association

A*

BLA	British Legal Association
BMA	British Medical Association
BTOG	British Transport Officers' Guild
CAWU	See APECCS
CBI	Confederation of British Industry
CBSA	Council of Bank Staff Associations
CCOA	County Court Officers' Association
CEF	Customs and Excise Confederation
CEPSA	Customs and Excise Preventive Staff Association
CHSE	Confederation of Health Service Employees
CIR	Commission on Industrial Relations
CPSA	Civil and Public Services Association
CSU	Civil Service Union
CWU	Chemical Workers' Union
DATA	See TASS
DE	Department of Employment (Formerly: Department of Employment and Productivity)
EETU–PTU	Electrical, Electronic, Telecommunication Union/Plumbing Trades Union
EPEA	Electrical Power Engineers' Association
Equity	British Actors' Equity Association
ESA	Engineer Surveyors' Association
FAA	The Film Artistes' Association
FBU	The Fire Brigades' Union
GLCSA	Greater London Council Staff Association
GMWU	National Union of General and Municipal Workers
GUALO	The General Union of Associations of Loom Overlookers
HVA	Health Visitors' Association
ILO	International Labour Organization
IPCS	Institution of Professional Civil Servants
IRSF	Inland Revenue Staff Federation
ISTC	Iron and Steel Trades Confederation
MLSA	Ministry of Labour Staff Association
MNALOA	Merchant Navy and Air Line Officers' Association

MOS	Managers' and Overlookers' Society
MPU	Medical Practitioners' Union
MU	Musicians' Union
NACODS	National Association of Colliery Overmen, Deputies and Shotfirers
NALGO	National and Local Government Officers' Association
NAS	National Association of Schoolmasters
NATKE	The National Association of Theatrical and Kine Employees
NATSOPA	See SOGAT
NBPI	National Board on Prices and Incomes
NCBLSA	National Coal Board Labour Staff Association
NFPW	National Federation of Professional Workers
NGA	National Graphical Association
NIRC	National Industrial Relations Court
NUBE	National Union of Bank Employees
NUCO	National Union of Co-operative Officials
NUCT	National Union of Commercial Travellers
NUIW	National Union of Insurance Workers
NUJ	National Union of Journalists
NUM	National Union of Mineworkers
NUPBPW	See SOGAT
NUPE	National Union of Public Employees
NUR	National Union of Railwaymen
NUT	National Union of Teachers
PFTA	Professional Footballers' and Trainers' Association
POA	Prison Officers' Association
POEU	Post Office Engineering Union
POMSA	Post Office Management Staffs' Association
RBSATEA	The Retail Book, Stationery and Allied Trades Employees' Association
RCN	Royal College of Nursing
REOU	Radio and Electronic Officers' Union
RIBA	Royal Institute of British Architects
SOGAT	Society of Graphical and Allied Trades (Now: NATSOPA – National Society of Operative

	Printers, Graphical and Media Personnel; and SOGAT Division A, the former NUPBPW – National Union of Printing, Bookbinding and Paper Workers)
STCS	Society of Technical Civil Servants
SUPLO	Scottish Union of Power Loom Overlookers
TASS	Technical and Supervisory Section of Amalgamated Union of Engineering Workers (Formerly DATA – Draughtsmen's and Allied Technicians' Association)
TGWU	Transport and General Workers' Union
TSSA	Transport Salaried Staffs' Association
TUC	Trades Union Congress
TWU	The Tobacco Workers' Union
UIS	Union of Insurance Staffs
UKAPE	United Kingdom Association of Professional Engineers
UPW	Union of Post Office Workers
USDAW	Union of Shop, Distributive and Allied Workers
WGGB	Writers' Guild of Great Britain
YAPLO	Yorkshire Association of Power Loom Overlookers

1 · Introduction

This study is concerned with giving a broad survey of the present position of white-collar unionism in Britain. It first examines the size and growth trends of the white-collar labour force, and of the trade unions, staff associations and professional associations which they join. It next isolates and examines the effects of a number of key factors on the membership and nature of these organizations. Finally it examines the structure and activities of the three basic types.

There are several reasons for carrying out this form of study.

A main one is that the white-collar labour force is expanding, and by the next decade will account for over a half of the total labour force in Britain. The attitudes of this group to unionism will therefore be a fundamental determinant of the pattern of industrial relations in the future.

A second reason is that the field is one that is not comprehensively documented.

A third reason grows from the fact that the concept of a white-collar employee is a fairly arbitrary one, deriving mainly from historical precedent. This results in the situation where, for example, a group of girls operating certain machines in an open-plan office are classified as white-collar employees, while another group of girls operating machines of a similar complexity in a factory workshop are classified as blue-collar employees. Nevertheless the two groups typically show differences in attitudes and behaviours. A study of white-collar unionism can seek to explain this.

It is an intention of this work that by distinguishing the determinants of the membership and nature of white-collar unionism, the probable effects of the likely future environment on white-collar unionism will be able to be predicted. In so doing the study will indicate gaps in our knowledge, and so give pointers to areas where further research is needed.

2 · The Extent of White-Collar Unionism

DEFINITION OF WHITE-COLLAR LABOUR FORCE

To attempt rigorously to define the term 'white-collar labour force' would be a complex task, demanding as a prerequisite the definition of terms such as owner, employer, employee, professional, and the like. These terms are themselves complicated by the existence of several types of enterprises, and the fact that individuals can simultaneously have more than one role. Rather than pursuing this complex, I propose to adopt a practical approach and to use terms in their common usage, but accepting the danger of differing interpretations I will attempt to make my meaning explicit.

The term 'labour force' will be applied to a group of employees; an employee being anyone who is paid for doing some work for some other person or for an organization. It will then be assumed that the labour force can be categorized into two groups, white-collar and blue-collar. Since there are numerous occupations, each one measurable on multiple criteria, this categorization must necessarily be a coarse and arbitrary process. It is particularly so since the basis of division is not job content, or size of payment, or even 'clean' and 'dirty' jobs; it is a historic division.

In the nineteenth century, the very few clerks that there were had a special relationship with their employers and could validly be distinguished from the mass of workpeople. But to this group were added, as time progressed, the growing numbers of office workers, shop assistants, technicians and the like, so that now the white-collar labour force can be taken as consisting, but not exclusively, of employees in the following categories:

administrators, managers, executives, supervisors, professionals, scientists, technologists, technicians, draughtsmen, 'creative occupations' – e.g. artists, entertainers, musicians, footballers; clerical and administrative workers, shop assistants, salesmen, commercial travellers; and other persons with a similar job content to the above, whether employed in public or private industry.

The terms manual and non-manual, and works and staff, are commonly used as synonymous with blue-collar and white-collar. Since all jobs have some element of both manual and non-manual skills, the first pair of terms are confusing; while the second pair of terms refer to conditions of employment given by employers, the differences of which are beginning to break down now. I therefore choose to use the terms 'blue-collar' and 'white-collar'.

STATISTICS OF WHITE-COLLAR LABOUR FORCE

Currently the white-collar labour force accounts for about 40 per cent of the total labour force, and this percentage is growing. While the number of white-collar employees increased by 176 per cent between 1911 and 1966, the number of blue-collar employees increased by only 5 per cent, although the downward trend in absolute numbers of the blue-collar labour force has been reversed since 1961.[1] Similar movements are taking place in other countries.[2]

Table 2.1 shows the breakdown of the white-collar labour force industrially, and growth trends. There is a decline in a

[1] See G. S. Bain and R. Price, 'Union Growth and Employment Trends in the U.K., 1964–70', *BJIR*, November 1972, pp. 368–9, Table 1, for further details. Bain excludes managers in private industry from his definition of white-collar employees, and therefore all his figures quoted in this study are a very slight underestimate.
[2] In the United States, white-collar employees now outnumber blue-collar employees. Throughout Western Europe and Japan the proportion of white-collar employees is rising. See A. Sturmthal, 'White-Collar Unions – A Comparative Essay', in A. Sturmthal (ed.), *White-Collar Trade Unions* (Urbana, Ill., University of Illinois Press, 1967), pp. 367–8.

number of basic industries, e.g. mining, and in older manu-facturing industries, e.g. textiles, which is being offset by expansion in newer manufacturing industries, e.g. chemicals, and professional services. Broadly speaking the declining industries have a much lower proportion of white-collar employees than have the expanding industries, although in both the proportion of white-collar employees is increasing. This is due to technical innovation leading to changes in the types of skills required.

Occupationally, the overall composition of the white-collar labour force is of clerks making up 34½ per cent, salesmen and shop assistants 16 per cent, lower professionals and technicians 17 per cent, managers and administrators 16 per cent, higher professionals 9 per cent, and foremen and inspectors 8 per cent [1]. In manufacturing industry overall, clerks make up about 46 per cent of the white-collar labour force, and in some industries, such as engineering and electrical, scientists, technologists and technicians make up some 29 per cent [2].

Of the six white-collar groups noted above, managers and administrators have shown the greatest growth over recent years, having increased by 19 per cent between 1961 and 1966 [3]. These categories do not distinguish scientific and technical occupations where there have been rapid growths. Between 1961 and 1966, the number of scientists and engineers increased by 28 per cent [4]. Recently there has been a decline in the demand for male clerical workers.[1]

Women make up about 46 per cent of the white-collar labour force (compared with 36 per cent of the total labour force) and this proportion is growing.[2] The average annual increase in the number of women white-collar employees is 3·3 per cent compared with the growth rate of 2·3 per cent for all white-collar employees [5]. Reasons for this increase include a more favourable social attitude towards working women, smaller families and labour-saving devices in the home, with the additional factor of the pull of high overall employment [6].

---

[1] Infra, pp. 37–45.
[2] Bain and Price, op. cit., p. 370, Table 3; figures for 1966. This is also the trend in other industrial nations. See Sturmthal, op. cit., pp. 372–3.

TABLE 2.1

Composition of the labour force by industry, showing the number of white-collar workers, and the growth trends.

Industry	Number employed (1971) (1)	White-collar employees as % of total (1971) (2)	Approximate annual % change in total number employed (3)	Approximate annual % change in number of white-collar employees (3)
Food, Drink, Tobacco	828,900	24·3	+1·2	+3·1
Chemicals and Allied Industries (4)	525,800	39·9	+1·7	+2·4
Metal Manufacture	569,100	24·6	−0·7	+2·0
Engineering and Electrical Goods	2,219,100	34·2	−1·0	−0·3
Shipbuilding and Marine Engineering	193,400	21·4	+0·4	+0·8
Vehicles	824,200	29·1	+0·8	+1·0
Metal Goods	621,700	22·4	+3·4	+5·7
Textiles	624,100	17·3	−3·1	−0·3
Leather, Leather Goods and Fur	51,900	17·5	−1·8	−1·4
Clothing and Footwear	473,900	12·8	−1·1	−0·5
Bricks, Pottery, Glass, Cement, etc.	326,800	22·2	−2·1	+2·4
Timber, Furniture, etc.	295,000	21·1	−2·2	+1·7
Paper, Printing, Publishing	627,100	30·1	−0·3	+2·7
Other Manufacturing Industries	346,700	24·2	+0·3	+0·8
Total Manufacturing	8,528,200	27·1	−0·3	+1·2
Agriculture, Forestry, Fishing	344,500	5·4	−5·6	+1·5
Mining and Quarrying	404,700	12·0	−6·3	−2·7
Construction	1,242,500	17·4	−5·5	−2·8
Gas, Electricity, Water	372,300	34·3	−3·6	−2·2
Transport and Communication	1,564,000	19·6	−0·4	−0·3
Distributive Trades	2,582,200	36·7 (5)	−2·3	−2·9 (5)
Professional and Scientific Services	2,082,800	66·8		

Industry	Number employed (1971) (1)	White-collar employees as % of total (1971) (2)	Approximate annual % change in total number employed (3)	Approximate annual % change in number of white-collar employees (3)
Insurance, Banking, Finance and Business Services	971,300	90·7	+15·3	+16·0
Miscellaneous Services	1,794,000	14·9	−4·9	−9·2
Public Administration and Defence	1,416,300	42·4	+0·3	+1·4
OVERALL TOTAL	22,027,000	40·7	−0·9	+11·3

Notes:
(1) Manufacturing Industries, Mining, etc., Construction, Gas, etc., at April; remainder at June.
(2) Figures for non-manufacturing industries include proprietors and employers (other than farmers) and are therefore a slight overestimate.
(3) Average for the years 1968–71.
(4) Including Coal and Petroleum Products.
(5) Excluding shop assistants.

Source: 'Number employed' from 'Employees in Employment: Industrial Analysis', *Department of Employment Gazette,* February 1972, pp. 196–7, Table 103.
'White-collar employees as a % of total' from 'Administrative, Technical and Clerical Workers in Manufacturing Industries', *Department of Employment Gazette,* July 1971, p. 620; estimated from G. Routh, 'Trade Union Membership', in B. C. Roberts (ed.), *Industrial Relations – Contemporary Problems and Perspectives* (London, Methuen, 1968), p. 48, Table 6; and total estimated from G. S. Bain and R. Price, 'Union Growth and Employment Trends in the U.K., 1964–70', *BJIR,* November 1972, pp. 368–9, Table 1.
'Annual % change in total number employed' calculated from *Department of Employment Gazette,* February 1972, pp. 196–7, Table 103.
'Annual % change in number of white-collar employees' calculated using 'Administrative, Technical and Clerical Workers in Manufacturing Industries', *Employment and Productivity Gazette,* July 1968, p. 557; Routh, op. cit., p. 48, Table 6; *Department of Employment Gazette,* February 1972, pp. 196–7, Table 103.

Industrially, women are concentrated in the service industries, and they form a majority of the total labour force in the distributive trade and make up about 45 per cent of those employed in insurance, banking and finance [7]. They make up about 36 per cent of the white-collar labour force in manufacturing industries [8]. Occupationally, women make up about 69 per cent of the total number of clerks, and the majority of lower professionals (particularly school teachers and nurses), and shop assistants [9]. Although women only form 16·7 per cent of managers and administrators, this group, along with the clerical group, has shown the most rapid growth over recent years [10].

DEFINITION OF WHITE-COLLAR UNIONISM

Following Blackburn, I will define unionism as '... the existence and activity of any organization of employees in protecting and furthering the interests of its members, as employees' [11]. White-collar unionism is concerned with organizations composed in total or part of white-collar employees. These organizations include not only trade unions, but also staff associations and multi-purpose bodies such as professional associations which have influence in the employment field.

Trade unions can be defined as 'Associations of Employees, and Federations of such Associations, whether registered under the Trade Union Acts or not, known to the Department [of Employment] to include in their objects that of negotiating with employers with a view to regulating the wages and working conditions of their members'.[1] Since this definition covers the common usage of the term trade union, I will adopt it in preference to the statutory definition which includes only organizations of workers registered under the Industrial Relations Act 1971 [12]. A union consisting exclusively of white-collar employees will be referred to as a white-collar

---

[1] This was the definition used by the DE before the Industrial Relations Act 1971.

union, and one consisting of both blue-collar and white-collar employees as a partially white-collar union.

Staff associations[1] or house unions or company unions are bodies which exist to further the interests of their members but which are not '. . . an autonomous, self-contained union, but [are] to some extent dependent upon the goodwill of the employer, and perhaps [have] some financial assistance from him' [13]. They are confined almost exclusively to white-collar employees.

Professional associations are formed by members of a profession. A profession is extremely difficult to define, and the most common approach has been to define attributes which characterize professions [14]. The main shortcoming of this approach is that it makes use of static definitions to describe something as dynamic as occupational change, for there is a constant trend towards professionalism by many occupations who regard professionalism as having high status. I will therefore consider an occupation to be a profession if it claims this status because its members will then, presumably, exhibit professional behaviour.

Four broad basic types of professional associations can be distinguished. These are the 'Prestige Association', the 'Study Association', the 'Qualifying Association' and the 'Occupational Association', which can be sub-divided into the 'Co-ordinating Association' and the 'Protective Association' [15]. Any one professional association might combine several of these functions with differing emphases.

Of the above, the protective association, and to a lesser extent the co-ordinating association, have as their major concern the protection of the occupational interests of their members; while the qualifying association, through control of entry to a profession, has influence in the employment field. These are therefore included under the definition of white-collar unionism.

---

[1] It should be noted that all bodies called staff associations do not fit this definition, e.g. Ministry of Labour Staff Association is an independent, TUC-affiliated, trade union. Other bodies, which are simply social clubs, are sometimes called staff associations. They are excluded from this discussion.

MEASUREMENT OF WHITE-COLLAR UNIONISM

In that white-collar unionism is concerned with three broad categories of organizations, namely trade unions, staff associations and professional associations, with each category composed of numerous individual organizations, there is the problem of devising a comparative measure of unionism in different fields.

One possible measure of white-collar unionism is membership. Absolute membership figures in various fields are of some use in showing the extent of unionism, but a more useful approach to understanding the significance of unionism is to relate membership to the potential size of membership in the field through the term density. For any given field:

$$\text{Density} = \frac{\text{Actual Membership of Organization(s)}}{\text{Potential Membership of Organization(s)}} \times 100\%$$

The field can be an occupation or group of occupations, an industry or parts of an industry, a single firm, a geographical area, or any other similar grouping. Adoption of different fields depends on the purpose for which the information is required. An examination of a particular union requires taking its area of recruitment as the potential membership, while an examination of unionism within an industry requires taking that industry as the field.

Difficulties arise in computing the density of membership when there is more than one organization within a field, since the various organizations of white-collar unionism differ greatly both within and between the three broad categories. They cannot, therefore, be meaningfully combined together into an overall density figure. Membership is not, by itself, a sufficient measure of unionism, and a further measure is needed which can describe the nature of organizations.

One approach to this is to try to describe the character of unionism, i.e. the way in which organizations behave outwardly. This is the approach adopted by Blackburn who introduces the concept of unionateness. Unionateness is defined as the extent to which organizations regard collective bargaining as their main activity, are independent of employers for the purposes of negotiation, are prepared to be militant; and whether they declare themselves to be a trade union, are registered as a trade union, are affiliated to the TUC and are affiliated to the Labour party [16]. In other words Blackburn compares organizations falling under the definition of white-collar unionism with a traditional blue-collar union.

The strength of this approach is that it measures as similar, organizations that exhibit common outward characteristics. This paradoxically is also its weakness, in that the methods that an organization uses are the result of an interaction between its fundamental aims and the environment in which it operates. Differing mixes of these two factors can result in the same outward manifestations.

Detailed criticisms of this approach are that the first four variables distinguished fall on a scale, and rating of organizations on these variables must rest on judgment, while the final three variables, as will be discussed later, are open to differing interpretations.[1] There is no way, as yet, of giving weightings to the seven variables and of combining the rating of an organization on them into a single reading.

A better approach to measuring the nature of organizations would appear to be to concentrate on their aims. Similar organizations are ones with a similar scope and intensity of aims. This approach overcomes the problem of the environment affecting the methods used, but has the basic drawback that, by themselves, aims are merely a statement of intent and are non-verifiable.

To overcome this difficulty, aims could be considered along with achievements. Similar organizations are then those with similar aims and effectiveness, i.e. they have adapted equally well to their particular environments. This approach does not concentrate on the methods that organizations employ. For example, a white-collar union operating in a hostile environment in private industry must use different methods to win economic advancement for its members than must a professional

[1] Infra, pp. 83–94.

association representing fee-paid practitioners. Nevertheless a common aim and common success are measures of a common intensity of white-collar unionism.

A difficulty here is that of measurement. Organizations have a wide range of aims including, for example, economic advancement, influence over the making of decisions, and the provision of welfare benefits. How are these various factors to be weighed together? Then, within each factor there is the problem of lack of a common base-line to start measurement from, and the fact that some factors would be very difficult to quantify.

There is a further problem in the measurement of white-collar unionism. Whatever measure of the nature of organizations is adopted, it is evident that this has some relationship with membership, and that both measures are necessary to describe the significance of unionism in any particular field. Blackburn has quantified this relationship.[1]

In this study I am not going to pursue the task of finding an objective and quantifiable measure of the nature of unionism any further. In consequence of this, any attempt to find a quantifiable relationship between nature and membership is an unwarranted sophistication. Rather, I will adopt a qualitative approach. Within the body of the work the nature of the broad groups comprising white-collar unionism and the nature of certain individual organizations will be indicated.[2] However, the formal statistics of the extent of white-collar unionism will concentrate on membership.[3] The comparison of unionism between different fields must therefore rest more heavily on membership measurements than is theoretically desirable.

STATISTICS OF WHITE-COLLAR UNIONISM

There are currently some 280 white-collar unions and 20 partially white-collar unions [17], numerous staff associations,[4]

---

[1] Significance of Unionism in any field = Unionateness × Completeness. R. M. Blackburn, *Union Character and Social Class* (London, Batsford, 1967), pp. 14 and 43–6.

[2] Infra, Chapters 3 and 4.

[3] Infra, pp. 25–9.

[4] It is not possible to estimate the exact number. See *Minutes of Evidence of National Federation of Professional Workers to the Royal Commission on*

and some 500 professional associations of which a large proportion can be included under my definition of white-collar unionism [18].

Principal staff associations and professional associations are noted in Appendix 3. It has been estimated that the aggregate membership of all such bodies is about $2\frac{1}{4}$ million [19]. There is a downward trend in the number of staff associations and a general upward trend in the number of professional associations. Further general statistics on these bodies are not obtainable, so I will concentrate my discussion on trade unions.

White-collar and partially white-collar unions make up about half the total number of trade unions and about 32 per cent of total trade union membership [20]. Appendices 1 and 2 list the white-collar unions and principal partially white-collar unions affiliated to the TUC, and Appendix 3 includes some of the principal non-affiliated white-collar unions.

Table 2.2 shows that white-collar membership of unions is increasing, while blue-collar membership remains fairly static. Appendices 1 and 2 show this trend in more detail. Table 2.2 also shows that since 1964 the growth in white-collar union membership has more than just kept pace with the increasing white-collar labour force, and that the density of membership has risen to 38 per cent. This compares with 52·7 per cent for blue-collar workers.[1] However, including staff associations and professional associations along with trade unions gives an overall density of about 50 per cent for white-collar unionism. This figure is of use only in showing that white-collar employees are as likely to be members of some organization of unionism as are blue-collar employees.[2]

A breakdown by industries of the membership of trade

Trade Unions and Employers' Associations (London, HMSO, 1966), p. 1070; and G. S. Bain, *Trade Union Growth and Recognition*, Research Paper 6 of the Royal Commission on Trade Unions and Employers' Associations (London, HMSO, 1967), p. 93.

[1] With the exception of Japan, all industrial nations show a lower proportion of white-collar employees than blue-collar employees organized into unions. See Sturmthal, op. cit., pp. 375–6.

[2] Further than this it is meaningless because of the different natures of the organizations of white-collar unionism.

TABLE 2.2

Trade union membership and density, 1964–1970

Type of employees in trade union	Number of members			Density of membership (%)						
	1964	1970	% change	1964 Male	Female	Total	1970 Male	Female	Total	Change
White-Collar	2,623,000	3,531,000	+34·6	34·9	22·6	29·0	42·9	32·4	38·0	+9·0
Blue-Collar	7,442,000	7,459,000	+0·2	60·3	28·0	51·0	60·8	32·9	52·7	+1·7
Total (All Unions)	10,065,000	10,990,000	+9·2			45·5			48·1	+2·6

Source: Number of Members from G. S. Bain and R. Price, 'Union Growth and Employment Trends in the U.K., 1964–70', BJIR, November 1972, p. 378, Table 10.
Density of Membership from ibid, pp. 378–9, Table 11.

unions by white-collar employees must rest largely on estimates. This is because the membership of individual unions generally sprawls across a variety of industries and occupations, and because only in manufacturing industry do the government's manpower figures give the number of white-collar employees. Table 2.3 shows two sets of estimates which agree reasonably well. They serve to show the concentration of membership in the public sector, where some 80 per cent of white-collar employees are members of trade unions, compared with about 10 per cent in private manufacturing industry.[1]

In manufacturing industries a more exact breakdown is available. This shows that white-collar membership of unions varies from a density of 23 per cent in the paper, printing and publishing industry to 0·3 per cent in the leather and fur, and clothing and footwear industries.[2] The growth of union membership among white-collar employees has been more than twice as great in manufacturing industries as in the economy as a whole. Growth has been most rapid in recent years, and membership in manufacturing industries grew by 44 per cent from 1955 to 1964, although the density of membership over this period only grew by 2 to 3 per cent [21].

Statistics of white-collar membership of trade unions by occupations are also largely confined to manufacturing industries. The overall highest membership density is among draughtsmen, who average 48·7 per cent, and the lowest among scientists and technologists, who average 5·3 per cent [22]. Outside of manufacturing industries it has been estimated that 80 per cent of engineers employed in local government are trade union members [23], and that the growth rate of union membership in the public sector is higher among scientific and managerial grades than among clerical and supervisory staff [24].

Women white-collar employees, as shown in Tables 2.2 and 2.3, have a lower overall density of union membership than men

[1] Internationally, white-collar employees in public employment show a higher degree of organization than those in private enterprises. See Sturmthal, op. cit., pp. 377–8.
[2] Figures are for 1964. Full details of manufacturing industries in Bain, op. cit., p. 27, Table 16.

TABLE 2·3

Estimated trade union membership among white-collar employees, by industry

Industry	Membership density (%) Estimate (a) December 1962			Estimate (b) 1960	Estimated change in density (%) 1948–1960
	Men	Women	Total	Total	
Distributive Trades	16	11	13	15	−2
Insurance, Banking, Finance	40	22	32	31 (1)	+11
Educational Services	58	32	40	50	−11 (3)
All other professional and scientific services	25	18	20	–	–
Cinemas, Theatres, Sport, Radio, etc.	55	20	38	39	+4
National Government Services	66	73	68	83	+19
Local Government Services	57	100	70	84	+16
Manufacturing	–	–	–	12 (2)	–
Total	36	25	31	–	–

Notes:
(1) For NUBE only.
(2) For 1963.
(3) Decrease due to rise in number of non-union ancillary staff.

Source: Estimate (a) from G. Routh, 'White-Collar Unions in the United Kingdom', in A. Sturmthal (ed.), *White-Collar Trade Unions* (Urbana, Ill., University of Illinois Press, 1967), p. 170, Table 2.

Estimate (b) and Change in Density from G. S. Bain, *Trade Union Growth and Recognition*, Research Paper 6 of the Royal Commission on Trade Unions and Employers' Associations (London, HMSO, 1967), p. 20, Table 13.

except in the public sector. Table 2.2. shows that from 1964 to 1970, the density of union membership among female white-collar employees rose by 9·8 per cent, compared with an 8 per cent increase for males. Figures giving a breakdown by industries show that from 1960 to 1966 inclusive, the largest growth took place in insurance, banking and finance, where the total union membership among women increased by 64 per cent [25].

Figures on white-collar membership of unions by geographic regions are available only for manufacturing industry. These show that the density of membership is highest in Wales and to a lesser extent in northern and north-western England, and lowest in London and the south-east [26].

3 · *Factors Affecting White-Collar Unionism*

SOCIAL STATUS

A basic factor in the understanding of white-collar unionism is a knowledge of the kinds of people that white-collar employees typically are. The behaviour of any group can probably best be summarized in terms of the social class to which they belong. It is useful, therefore, to investigate the social status of white-collar employees.

The social status of an individual or group is their position in a hierarchy of prestige on various criteria. Status is based on each assessor's subjective opinion. The status of an occupation is generally assessed on criteria which include its economic position, education and training required for it, and the background of individuals entering it.

In the nineteenth century, the economic position of white-collar employees was generally superior to that of blue-collar employees. However, a relative decline in the income of lower skill white-collar employees, e.g. clerks, has led to a fall in status of this criterion.[1] A similar position exists with regard to education, since the general availability of free education has levelled out the difference between clerks, and other lower skilled white-collar employees, and blue-collar employees. Technical, scientific and professional occupations are maintaining high educational standards for entry, and high standards of training.

Whereas in the nineteenth century the majority of clerks came from middle-class families, the growth of the modern office has been accompanied by an increase in the proportion of clerks

[1] Infra, pp. 47–51.

whose social origin is working class [1]. The evidence is that by the middle of this century at least 50 per cent of clerks came from working-class homes [2]. This change is largely a result of increased educational opportunities leading children to enter a higher occupational class than their fathers, and is also due to the large increase in the employment of women in lower office positions. Although there is a general trend in the lower white-collar occupations towards increasing employment of people with a working-class background, there are still certain occupations where employees with a middle-class background predominate. A recent survey found that all but 5 per cent of male bank clerks came from middle-class homes [3].

In the scientific, professional and other higher skill white-collar occupations, the majority of employees have a traditional middle-class background. This is so even when free education is available to all, since a variety of factors act to give middle-class children a better chance of a longer and more successful education than children from working-class homes [4].

Thus, whereas in the past white-collar employees were confident of their superior social status to blue-collar employees and were sure of their relative standing within the white-collar group, the result of the changes outlined above has been to make many of them unsure of their social status [5]. The situation is blurred further by a general breakdown in the traditional distinctions between different classes [6]. In some occupations there is a fairly general feeling that their social status has fallen [7], while in other occupations individuals show widely differing perceptions of their social status [8].

A fairly common view of the effect of social status on white-collar unionism is that white-collar employees see themselves as of higher status than blue-collar employees, and that this 'snobbish' outlook makes them avoid patterns of behaviour which might identify them with blue-collar employees, e.g. joining a trade union [9]. This view is a gross oversimplification. It fails to recognize the differing perceptions of status among white-collar employees, or to explain the pattern of unionism existing among them.

Social status in fact has little direct effect on the membership density of unionism [10]. Thus high-status journalists and low-status railway clerks both exhibit a high density of unionism, while low-status industrial clerks exhibit a low density of unionism.[1]

The social status of white-collar employees does, however, influence the nature of unionism. It can be put forward as a general hypothesis that the higher the overall perceived status of a white-collar occupation, the greater the likelihood that unionism, if it exists at all, will take the form of an organization which outwardly accepts the legitimacy of the existing power structure within the employing enterprise, and the less likely is there to be an organization which seeks to change the existing power structure. Within any occupation, the higher that individuals perceive their own status, the more likely are they to join the former sort of organization if a choice of organizations exists; or, if there is no choice of organizations, then they will try to influence the one existing organization, if they join it, to adopt a favourable attitude towards the existing power structure.

Professional associations accept, in general, the claims to legitimacy of the ruling group, though this in no way prevents them from seeking to protect their own interests. Staff associations fall in a similar category. They typically rely on the goodwill of the employer to achieve their goals, and do not generally question 'managerial prerogative'. Unlike most professional associations, some staff associations may be little concerned with salaries, seeing them as a matter for independent bargaining between employer and employee, and they may be unable to bring pressure to bear on employers. Trade unions, in general, bargain with employers on behalf of employees, and by so doing are expressing a conflict of interest.

There is considerable evidence in support of the above hypothesis. Railway clerks, who are predominantly from the working class and are low paid and little skilled, and can therefore be classified of low social status, have formed in TSSA a trade union which acts very much like a traditional blue-collar union. Bank clerks, in contrast, have fairly high

[1] Other factors account for this. See infra, pp. 34–65.

social status, and have joined either NUBE, which is a fairly non-militant union, or the staff associations. Within banking, the higher an individual's perceived social status, the more likely is he to have joined a staff association rather than NUBE, or to have joined neither [11].

Professional engineers traditionally perceive their status as high. Few of them join trade unions, and the minority who do join show very moderate attitudes and try to mould the union into acting in a moderate way [12]. Until the recent founding of UKAPE, most engineers who joined an organization joined the Engineers' Guild, which is a professional association placing emphasis on co-operation with management [13].[1] Among the minority of members of the Guild who do favour collective bargaining, there are more engineers who have had a part-time technical college education than ones with a full-time university education [14].

As white-collar employees' perceptions of the social status of their occupation alters, so do their attitudes to unionism. An example is given by the teachers who, in the face of falling economic position and dissatisfaction over employment conditions and their degree of autonomy, shifted the emphasis of the NUT from a professional association to a militant trade union [15]. A survey reveals that the majority of teachers thought that they would lose public sympathy by striking [16]. They were, however, willing to sacrifice status on one factor in order to gain it on another. At the same time a minority of teachers have shown their concern for professionalism and status by breaking away from the NUT to form the Professional Association of Teachers, a non-militant body.

The BMA provides an example of an organization which maintains the image of a professional association to the public, and indeed to many of its members, in keeping with the status of the medical profession. It is, nevertheless, highly active in matters directly concerned with furthering its members' interests, and is therefore effective in maintaining their high status.

[1] UKAPE promises to behave in a similar way to the BMA, see infra, pp. 111–21.

The weight of evidence is in favour of a provisional acceptance of the above hypothesis on the effect of social status on white-collar unionism. It seems that all white-collar employees are concerned with protecting and furthering their own interests but that the most appropriate and effective methods for doing this vary with their perceived social status. The higher-status white-collar employees are naturally the group most concerned about status, and as an aid to maintaining this they normally seek to act in a professional manner in order to enhance their status. However, should such methods prove ineffective, then they are willing to turn to trade unions '. . . as something to be used rather than something in which to believe' [17]. When NUBE held its first major strike in 1968, membership increased by 20,000 within a few weeks as bank employees saw a way of restoring their fallen status through militancy [18].

The relationship between social status and the nature of unionism needs to be constantly reviewed in the light of the changing environment. As the pluralistic frame of reference becomes more generally accepted, high-status employees become more favourably inclined towards union activities.[1] This trend involves a movement of the whole scale of unionism rather than a relative displacement. An example is shown by the Engineers' Guild, where more members from the public than from the private sector favour collective bargaining, since in the public sector collective bargaining is generally accepted as normal and acceptable for senior employees [19].

EMPLOYMENT OF WOMEN

Women make up about 46 per cent of the white-collar labour force, compared with about 36 per cent of the total labour force, and this proportion is growing.[2] It is therefore important to note any special characteristics of the employment of women having a bearing on white-collar unionism.

With the exception of the public sector of the economy,

---

[1] See infra, pp. 56–7, for explanation of pluralistic frame of reference.
[2] Supra, pp. 17 and 20. This gives the industrial and occupational breakdown of women white-collar employees.

women show an overall lower density of union membership than men.[1] No separate figures for the female membership of staff associations and professional associations are available. Within organizations of white-collar unionism women typically take a less militant attitude than men. A survey among teachers, for example, showed this [20]. Such attitudes and behaviour are a result both of factors typically existing in the employment environment of women and of special characteristics of women as employees.

In manufacturing industries, at least, most women work in the smaller establishments, and this lower degree of employment concentration is a contributory factor to their lower density of union membership [21].[2]

Many, but not all, women marry and have children, with consequent breaks in employment. They are therefore regarded by many employers as a temporary and unstable part of the labour force. It is this factor, coupled with a traditional and lingering prejudice that women are inferior to men, that largely accounts for the typical work situation of women: they tend to do lower grade work than men, they have fewer chances of promotion and are less well paid [22]. In turn, this typical work situation serves to give women low commitment to work and so they exhibit high labour turnover. (The average labour turnover for women is almost twice as great as for men [23].) A vicious circle is therefore set up, since the evidence reinforces the employers' views that women are an unstable part of the labour force and not worth training for higher responsibility jobs.

Their rapid labour turnover results in women having little chance to appreciate the particular problems of a given workplace, and so to establish themselves in a union branch. It also precludes them from standing for office since they have not satisfied the qualifying period [24]. The fact that many women are playing a dual role of housewife and employee means that they have little time to devote to the work of an organization of unionism. It also means that they will be less outward looking on average than men, and therefore less aware of their economic

[1] Supra, Tables 2.2 and 2.3.
[2] Infra, pp. 51–4.

and social standing relative to other work groups. Thus women tend to be less dissatisfied with their position and less interested in wider issues of concern to large groups of employees.

The attitude of women towards white-collar unionism is accentuated by two related characteristics. One is the fact that women are generally more conservative than men, and the other is the development, particularly among older women, of a high degree of what they call loyalty to their employer. Thus, particularly when they work in close contact with him, the attitude of their employer towards unionism will be a crucial determinant of their own.[1]

The factors above explain why, among those who join some organization of white-collar unionism, women are fairly prone to join staff associations [25]. Such organizations typically are non-militant, recognize no conflict with their employer, and are inward looking.[2]

There is one further factor affecting the attitudes of women to white-collar unionism, and that is the behaviour of the organizations themselves towards women. Typically they are quite unattractive to women members. There is still prejudice in some areas against permitting women to discuss anything but their own problems, and this leads to diminished opportunities for participation. Thus NUPE, with 51 per cent female membership, sent a delegation of twenty-four men and no women to the 1967 TUC. This is not universal, however. In the public sector, where women do have conditions of employment and prospects equal to those of men, as is largely the case in teaching and in the Civil Service, then they show a density of union membership equal to that of men [26]. In this area, too, as among white-collar unions in general, unions show less discrimination against women. For example, NALGO, NUT and APECCS all have women members on their executive councils and have had women presidents.

In the future, as the employment environment of women in general changes, so will their behaviour towards white-collar unionism. Increasingly women are gaining equal rights, and the

---

[1] Infra, pp. 56–61.
[2] Infra, pp. 105–8.

Government has passed the Equal Pay Act 1970 which will ensure them equal pay by the end of 1975. This will serve to give women a higher commitment to work and a higher propensity to join organizations of unionism. Against this trend must be set the fact that an increasing number of married women are working – and in 1965 they made up 54 per cent of all women in employment [27]. These women are playing a dual role which will inevitably decrease their interest in unionism. However, married women are working longer than previously, and are joining unmarried women as more permanent members of the labour force [28].

The balance of these factors suggests that there will be a rise in the membership density of white-collar unionism by women. Evidence is given by the fact that between 1960 and 1966 the rise in women's membership accounted for 70 per cent of the total increase in trade union membership [29]. Nevertheless, the inherent characteristics of women and their family responsibilities make it likely that they will continue to play only a small part within the organizations, so that the nature of unionism will continue to be strongly influenced by men.

LEVEL OF EMPLOYMENT

Of the external factors acting on white-collar employees, the level of employment in the economy might appear to be a basic one affecting unionism. In fact a TUC document has suggested that as far as the level of trade union membership is concerned it is the most important factor [30]. A fuller investigation of the effect of the level of employment on white-collar unionism therefore seems appropriate.

The post-war period has been overall one of high employment, but there have been variations in this picture in certain occupations and regions.[1] White-collar employees, as a group, have experienced high employment, as they occupy the expanding occupations. However, recently, total unemployment has risen to 3·7 per cent of the labour force while the number of

[1] See supra, pp. 16–17. Regionally, Ulster and Scotland show above average unemployment, and the south-east of England below average unemployment.

unfilled vacancies has fallen, and it seems likely that this upward trend in unemployment will continue, at least into the short-term future [31]. Although unemployment is largely concentrated among older men and among the unskilled, there is one white-collar group which is exhibiting relatively high unemployment. This group comprises male clerks, of whom 58,721 were out of work at September 1971, while there were only 4,224 unfilled clerical vacancies [32].

The general trend over the century has been for total trade union membership to increase in numbers during periods of rising employment, and to decrease with declining employment [33]. In the white-collar sector, overall high employment has been accompanied by an increase in the white-collar membership of unions and in the density of membership.[1]

Other than these general trends, there is a distinct lack of detailed evidence on the effect of the level of employment on the membership of white-collar unionism. The method for properly examining this question would be to note the percentage level of employment of white-collar employees over the years, and to note the aggregate membership of trade unions, staff associations and professional associations by white-collar employees over the same period. This latter set of figures would be divided by the total white-collar labour force at each period to give an overall density of unionism.[2] A statistical analysis would then be performed to find the correlation between the level of employment and the density of membership of white-collar unionism.

Alternatively, and perhaps more usefully, a similar analysis could be carried out separately for trade unions, for staff associations, and for professional associations. This would have more real meaning than the overall figure. For staff associations in particular this poses the practical difficulty of defining the scope of the field to be used for calculating the level of employment and the potential membership. Furthermore, staff associations and professional associations are not typically

---

[1] Supra, Table 2.2.
[2] N.B. This density figure has no real meaning, since it ignores the differing nature of unionism. See supra, pp. 22–4.

considered as two unified groupings in the way that trade unions are, since they have no central body or unifying policies. However, for trade unions the analysis is both possible and meaningful.[1]

There is a similar lack of evidence on the effect of the level of employment on white-collar unionism on an occupational or industrial basis. It would be extremely difficult to carry this analysis out since to do so would involve defining the boundary of the occupation or industry, finding the percentage of unemployed within that boundary over the years and the membership of the organizations of unionism within that area. Probably it would be most meaningful to do a separate analysis for trade unions, staff associations and professional associations because of the absence of a quantifiable measure of the nature of unionism which would enable their memberships to be combined together. There still remains the practical problem, particularly among unions, of finding the total membership in any area, since the structure of unions typically follows neither a wholly occupational nor an industrial structure, and there is considerable overlapping among them.[2]

In the absence of such an analysis, it is necessary to fall back on some looser evidence. A comparison of Tables 2.1 and 2.3 (pp. 18–19 and 28) shows that there appears to be no apparent connection between the rate of growth in an industry, and with it a higher level of employment, and a change in density of union membership. What is probably the case is that all things being equal, an industrial or occupational grouping of white-collar employees enjoying high employment will show a higher density of union membership than one showing high unemployment, but generally all things are not equal, and other factors act to influence unionism.[3]

The general connection between the level of employment and union membership can be explained by the fact that the higher the level of unemployment, the stronger the position of the

---

[1] To carry it out is beyond the scope of this study, which aims at giving a broad survey over the whole field of white-collar unionism.
[2] Infra, pp. 66–70.
[3] Supra, pp. 30–7; and infra, pp. 41–65.

employer relative to the employee. The latter, in order to retain his present job or obtain another in the scarce market, is careful to do nothing to antagonize his employer, which may well include not joining a trade union. This applies particularly where unions are relatively weak, which has been their traditional position, particularly among white-collar employees.

This explanation is only relevant where the employer is antagonistic towards the organization of white-collar unionism. It is therefore not applicable to trade unions in the public sector, or to staff associations or professional associations in general.

In times of high employment, the employee is in a stronger position relative to the employer, and this provides all organizations of unionism with their best opportunity to be effective in influencing employers, and therefore of being most attractive to prospective members. This is a reason for the general trend that has been observed in union membership movements, and it leads to the prediction that there are similar movements in the memberships of staff associations and of professional associations other than qualifying associations. The extent to which white-collar employees join such organizations will depend on the extent to which they see them as effective.

The level of employment also has an effect on the nature of unionism. Trends can be viewed at two levels. High employment, coupled with general satisfaction on other factors, '. . . will induce the organization to be concerned with professional standards rather than the immediate terms of employment' [34], since this is seen as the best way of furthering its members' interests. This is not the normal situation, however, and high employment coupled with some dissatisfaction about conditions of employment leads to increasingly direct and determined activity to improve these conditions. Evidence is given by the trends in TASS, the staff associations in banking, NUT, and BMA in recent years.[1] This can be explained by the fact that high employment leads to high membership and places the organization in a relatively strong position to take effective action to help its members.

[1] Infra, pp. 99, 108–11 and 115–18.

In the past, periods of relatively high unemployment served to make organizations of white-collar unionism fairly passive and inactive. This was partly because they feared discriminatory action by employers, as was the case for unions in private industry, and partly because the environment was not conducive to successful action. However, in the future, as white-collar unionism grows increasingly strong, rising unemployment will provide an incentive for increasing membership and activity. This is because the threat of unemployment or diminished promotional opportunity faces white-collar employees with a situation of great uncertainty. Strong unionism will offer the promise of protection from this uncertainty.

Evidence that this is likely to happen is shown by the fact that where, at the moment, white-collar unionism is strong, the organizations take steps to minimize fluctuations in the level of employment of their members. They do this through restrictions in the entry to occupations, as in the case of trade unions operating a form of closed shop or professional associations carrying out a qualifying function, and through restrictions in the way that their members will work, as in the case of restrictive practices operated by both trade unions and professional associations.[1]

Thus, in the future, an increasing and a falling level of employment will both be conducive to a high membership of unionism, but only to the extent that organizations are effective in protecting and furthering the interests of their members. However, the two situations require different tactics, and will thus influence the nature of unionism.

TECHNICAL CHANGE

Technical change is taking place more rapidly now than at any period in the past. Both envelope curves, which represent the advancement in any technical sphere over time, and diffusion curves, which plot the intervals taken for new technologies to diffuse broadly through society over time, are exponential [35]. Technical change is bringing about differences in the relative

[1] Infra, pp. 102–3 and 112–13.

B*

growth of industries, and of occupations within industries.[1] Its overall effect is to increase the number of white-collar employees.

At establishment level, technical change is one of the factors leading to concentration of production in larger units, since only then can the full advantages of new methods be realized. Within establishments mechanization and automation, besides leading to an obvious increase in the numbers of technologists and technicians employed, is having a deleterious effect on clerical workers.[2] The need for large numbers of employees for the routine processing of data inevitably leads to the de-skilling of some jobs. Typically, following the demands of the machinery, these are centralized and work under social and physical conditions similar to those in a factory. There are diminished upward promotional opportunities for lower clerical employees, as the gap between them and managers grows [36]. At the same time, advanced mechanization and automation is creating a demand for small numbers of skilled personnel to fill new and more interesting jobs.

Technical change, as a factor, is not really quantifiable, and so figures of its effect on white-collar unionism are not obtainable and this discussion must remain qualitative in nature. In that technical change brings about an increase in the white-collar labour force, it creates the potential for an increase in the overall membership of white-collar unionism. Whether membership does rise, and the effects such a rise might have on the nature of unionism, depend on a variety of circumstances.

The initial effect of technical change on any group of employees is to give rise to a feeling of uncertainty and a sense of insecurity. This reaction is typical whether the medium- or long-term consequences of the change turn out to be to the detriment or to the advantage of the group. Thus change presents a threat, in the face of which many white-collar employees join organizations of white-collar unionism as a means of protection.

The standing of a professional, for example, is built upon his

---

[1] Supra, pp. 16–20.
[2] Between 1964 and 1967 the number of computers installed or on order almost doubled from 1,100 to over 2,000.

understanding of a body of knowledge and the system in which
this operates, and on the confidence of the public in his ability.
Any change might pose a threat to his standing by taking away
part of his traditional duties, as would be the case, say, with the
introduction of computers into the field of medical diagnosis.
The membership of professional associations therefore increases
in the face of change, and the associations become increasingly
active in protecting the interests of their members and in
particular in attempting to enforce restrictive practices.[1]

The position is similar with trade unions. Many white-collar
employees fear that technical change will lead to redundancy,
and this fear is particularly acute among office workers. It has
been estimated that the introduction of computers will eliminate
some 300,000 office jobs by 1974, though the main effect in fact
will be to offset the growing shortage of office workers, not to
produce redundancies [37]. Although this may be true on an
overall basis, individuals still feel insecure in their own jobs and
are aware that computerization means that jobs which would
have appeared in the future, now do not. They are also aware of
the rising unemployment among male clerical workers.[2] These
factors give clerical employees in particular an incentive to join
unions such as APECCS, which promise to fight for measures
to avoid redundancy and for opportunities for retraining [38].
Unions in this defensive situation may show outbursts of
militancy, but by and large they are in a weak market position
and must co-operate with employers in order to best serve their
members.

Draughtsmen, technicians and other groups often gain in the
long term through increased employment opportunity as a
result of technical change. However, in the short term it can be
threatening and may lead to redundancy. Thus these white-
collar employees have an incentive to join unions, and the
unions are able to exploit their strong market position to
protect their members. For example, ASTMS and TASS have
a record of militancy.[3]

[1] Infra, pp. 112–13.
[2] Supra, p. 38.
[3] Infra, p. 99.

When technical change is actually implemented, it can cause a great deal of disruption in an enterprise. At the extreme it can lead to a complete reorganization of departments, with much internal displacement and a need for retraining. This is very unsettling for employees, and makes them turn to unions and other organizations which aim to ensure that '. . . reasonable provision is made against adverse social effects . . .' [39]. In this situation some employees may join staff associations as a means of finding out what is going on, and perhaps also because these may be a channel of consultation on the issue.

The physical concentration of employees, which technical change often brings about, is typically accompanied by an impersonalization and standardization of their conditions of employment. These factors, coupled with blocked upward promotion, are an important cause of an increase in white-collar unionism.[1]

Technical change is bringing about alterations in the characteristics of the white-collar labour force. Mechanization is probably the most important single factor leading to the great growth in the numbers of women employed, and this has an effect on unionism.[2] Automation and mechanization are also giving power to new and unsophisticated groups, e.g. punch girls, and putting them in a position where, by industrial action, they have the ability to disrupt the working of an industrial enterprise. This seems a likely potential growth area for white-collar unionism.

An indirect result of technical change is that it is allowing more lateral mobility between industries, as jobs become more standardized. This applies to many types of white-collar employees and acts to make them less dependent on one employer or industry. Two main groups can be distinguished: one, which includes typists and punch operators, shows a very high labour turnover, while the second, which includes technologists, technicians and professionals who possess transferable skills, does not show such great instability in employment. Members of the former group typically do not join unions in great

[1] *Infra*, pp. 51–6.
[2] *Supra*, pp. 34–7.

numbers, since they are in a favourable market position and can change employer in an attempt to better their conditions rather than seeking to bring about improvements within a company. Coupled with this is the difficulty for unions to recruit and retain such mobile employees. Members of the latter group generally wish to secure improvement in terms and conditions of employment within their present employment and within the occupation in general, and therefore join trade unions and professional associations. They are able to do this, and to be fairly militant in furthering their claims, because they are not vulnerable to any employer discrimination.[1] For the same reasons these employees are less likely to join staff associations.

In the future, technical change will become increasingly rapid. It will exaggerate white-collar employees' sense of insecurity and increase the amount of disruption that they are subjected to. It is likely therefore to lead to increases in both the membership and the activity of white-collar unionism as employees seek to have some control over their environment.

TAKEOVERS AND MERGERS

In recent years there has been an increase in the number of takeovers and mergers, and they are taking place in all industries. The main reason for this is the increasing scale of investment and research needed for a business to remain competitive in the world market. At the same time, nationalization is bringing about larger concentrations of industrial power in the public sector, and here, also, large-scale reorganizations are taking place, e.g. in the National Health Service and in local government.

To investigate the effect of mergers and takeovers on white-collar unionism it would be necessary to extract figures of the number of employees involved in mergers and takeovers in a series of years, and to find the correlation between these figures and the overall membership of white-collar unionism. In addition, separate calculations could also be made by industry and occupation and for trade unions, staff associations and

[1] Infra, pp. 57–9.

professional associations. However, such an exercise is not really worth the effort. The blanket heading of takeovers and mergers conceals several separate variables, e.g. a rise in bureaucracy, which occur in individual cases to a greater or lesser extent, while the analysis is unable to take account of the differing nature of unionism, since there is no quantifiable measure of this factor. A better approach is to examine the effects of takeovers and mergers in particular cases.

The initial effect of a takeover is to give employees a sense of insecurity. They fear redundancy, since a takeover almost inevitably involves a rationalization of production, and this fear is particularly acute among managers. White-collar employees also feel apprehensive over possible changes in working methods or location. The effect of such fears is to make them join organizations of unionism which aim to ensure that they are kept informed of the position, and that employers do not solve rationalization problems at the employees' expense. In takeover situations, organizations for white-collar employees often change their nature and become increasingly active. A study of the takeover of an engineering firm confirms the effects on unionism [40].

Under these circumstances, employees are unlikely to join staff associations since these, as internal bodies, are viewed as being ineffective. The need is felt for an independent, broader-based organization, such as a union, which can protect the interests of employees in all the merging firms.

When takeovers and mergers are completed they result in larger enterprises, and often larger establishments, with an accompanying standardization and impersonalization of the conditions of employment. This causes an increase in white-collar unionism.[1]

For their part, some unions, e.g. ASTMS, APECCS, concentrate their recruiting effort on sectors of industry where there is a trend towards mergers and takeovers and the growth of larger units. They do this as a way of building up membership strength most rapidly, thereby wielding greater influence. There is no evidence, however, that this has any significant effects on

[1] Infra, pp. 52–4.

membership growth, since union recruitment campaigns can, at the most, act as a catalyst for membership growth [41].

A further consequence of takeovers is that they are bringing more companies under American ownership and control. One result is sometimes the creation of an employer-dominated staff association or 'company union' since 'American-owned concerns in particular are extremely reluctant to countenance trade union organization among staff employees...' [42]. Examples include Kodak and Gillette.

Mergers and takeovers will continue in the future, and firms will tend to become increasingly large. This is likely to lead to an increase in the membership of white-collar unionism, and also probably greater militancy as employees seek to have a say in their own destiny. There may be a decrease in the number of staff associations in some sectors as a result of provisions in the Industrial Relations Act 1971.[1]

PAY AND FRINGE BENEFITS

Of all the factors in the employment environment of white-collar employees, the level of remuneration might be thought to be an important determinant of their attitudes and behaviour towards unionism. As a group, white-collar employees have a higher average income than blue-collar employees [43]. There are, however, some white-collar workers, e.g. clerks, shop assistants, who are much lower paid than some blue-collar workers, e.g. dockers, car production-line workers.

Over the years there have been movements in the relative financial position of white-collar employees and blue-collar employees. Since the 1930s the former have, on the whole, suffered a relative decline and a survey revealed that the average manual worker with two children was about 55 per cent better off than immediately before World War II, while many white-collar employees were between 20 and 30 per cent worse off [44]. Many of the latter have suffered a decline not only in relation to the rising standard of living but also in real income terms, when allowance is made for the rising cost of living.

[1] Infra, pp. 63–4.

However, since 1956 this decline has been largely halted, and quite a few white-collar employees have increased their standard of living from that date [45]. From 1956 to 1967, average salary earnings rose by 94·7 per cent compared with a 92·3 per cent rise for all manual workers but since this date wages have increased at a slightly higher rate than salaries [46].

Two points must be borne in mind when comparing the pay of blue-collar and white-collar employees. Firstly, the former typically work longer hours, and supplement their basic rate with overtime and bonus payments, which means that their earnings fluctuate. Thus from 1956 to 1967, the average weekly basic rate for blue-collar employees increased by only 64·2 per cent [47]. Secondly, whereas most blue-collar employees reach the peak of their earning capacity early in their careers, many white-collar employees are on incremental scales. Individual white-collar employees can therefore maintain or improve their real income, even though the average real income of the occupation as a whole might be deteriorating. Thus, for a Civil Service Executive Officer, the real income of the class rose by a factor of 1·16 from 1947 to 1960, while that of any individual rose by a factor of 2·71 [48].

White-collar employees do, on the whole, enjoy superior fringe benefits to blue-collar employees [49]. For example, a Department of Employment survey revealed that at April 1970, 91·6 per cent of male and 82·3 per cent of female non-manual employees were covered by sick-pay schemes, compared with only 62·9 and 48·8 per cent respectively for male and female manual employees. For pension schemes the corresponding figures were 73·2 and 38·6 per cent for male and female non-manual employees, compared with 45·3 and 11·9 per cent for manual employees [50]. However, over recent years there has been a narrowing in the gap of the differences in fringe benefits paid to the two groups; sick pay and pension schemes for blue-collar employees are growing in number and quality, while a sizeable proportion of these workers now enjoy more than two weeks' paid annual holiday [51]. A recent White Paper revealed the Government intention that 'the normal job will be seen as providing not only a wage or salary but an earnings related pension as well' [52]. Nevertheless, since many fringe benefit schemes for blue-collar employees are based on their basic wage, rather than their average earnings, they are still somewhat inferior to those for white-collar employees.

As pay is a measurable factor, it is possible to investigate its effect on the membership of unionism. Within the white-collar labour force there has been found no demonstrable connection between absolute level of income and membership of trade unions [53]. Nor do those white-collar groups whose earnings relative to other white-collar groups have declined most show a higher density of union membership [54]. Similarly, there has been found no connection between the decline in payment differentials or fringe benefits of a white-collar group relative to blue-collar employees and density of union membership [55].

No comparable analyses have been made for professional associations or staff associations, although it would be possible to carry these out. It is likely that no connection would be found between the present level of income of various professions and the density of membership of professional associations, or between the relative movement of the level of income of a profession compared to other professions, white-collar groups and blue-collar groups, and the density of membership of professional associations. Staff associations are likely to show a similar pattern.

In the absence of a quantifiable measure of unionism it is not possible to carry out a statistical analysis of the effects of pay and fringe benefits on the nature of white-collar unionism. However, in that some organizations of high income employees are fairly militant, e.g. BALPA, BMA, while others are fairly passive, e.g. Engineers' Guild; and considering that some organizations of lower income employees are fairly militant, e.g. TSSA, while others are fairly passive, e.g. NUBE; it seems reasonable to assume that the absolute or relative level of income and fringe benefits of a group of white-collar employees bears little relationship to the nature of unionism.

The reason that differences in pay and fringe benefits do not distinguish differences in the extent and nature of white-collar unionism is that other factors in the work situation are more dominant determinants of behaviour.[1] The desire to maintain and improve their relative standing on pay and fringe benefits is common to all white-collar employees.

Nevertheless pay and fringe benefits are a general factor leading to an overall increase in white-collar unionism. Many white-collar employees are dissatisfied with their standing relative to other white-collar groups or to blue-collar employees. Thus a survey among teachers found that even considering the holidays, the great majority felt that they were not well paid and that their fringe benefits did not compare with those in industry [56]. Draughtsmen at the Coventry plant of Rolls-Royce have complained that they earn less than some skilled manual workers.

Many white-collar employees see the relative advance of the blue-collar labour force as due to strong organization, and so they seek to emulate this in order to defend their position. Unions such as ASTMS pledge themselves to increase differentials [57]. Professional associations seek to maintain salaries, and along with them status.

When a choice of organizations exists, those employees who are less dissatisfied with their salaries are more likely to join a professional association than a trade union [58]. The more dissatisfied that a group of workpeople are, and this rests on their perceptions rather than any objective measure of their position, the more active and militant they are likely to be. An example is the Junior Hospital Doctors' Association which broke away from the BMA. White-collar unionism is having some success in achieving its aims, and the halting of the relative decline in the terms and conditions of white-collar employees since the mid 1950s can be partly attributed to it.

In some circumstances, generous fringe benefits can influence the nature of white-collar unionism. Non-transferable pension rights can restrict labour mobility and so make employees more dependent on their employer, and less willing to antagonize him. At the present it is estimated that only 40 per cent of employees who leave early have the opportunity of retaining their pension rights, but the Government propose legislation to

[1] See particularly, infra, pp. 51–61.

ensure that those who leave before pension age are not so deprived [59]. Similarly, the fear of loss of pension rights can act as a disincentive to strike action; in fact Vickers-Armstrong (Shipbuilders) Ltd used the threat of discontinuance of their membership of the firm's pension scheme against striking draughtsmen in 1964.

The gap between the typical fringe benefits enjoyed by blue-collar employees and white-collar employees will probably continue to narrow, and groups will continue to compare their pay position unfavourably with those of various reference groups. Thus pay and fringe benefits will remain a general background factor leading to the growth of white-collar unionism but will not, by themselves, act as a stimulus to this growth or distinguish the relative growth between and within occupations and industries.

WORK ENVIRONMENT

Aspects of the work environment of white-collar employees, and particularly the physical conditions under which they work, the systems of management and administration to which they are subjected, the type of work that they do, and their opportunities for promotion, are significant factors affecting white-collar unionism.

The traditional image of the typical white-collar employee is of a person working in a small office in close personal contact with his employer. In some clerical and scientific posts this image is still valid. Small work groups containing a hierarchy of skill carry out a specialized function for a manager. Employees at the same level in the hierarchy are separated from each other by the authority structure of the organization and by their lack of common skills [60].

However, there is a general and continuing trend for white-collar employees of all types to be employed in larger groups containing employees of the same grade, and to be separated from their superiors. This is following the trend towards larger enterprises [61]. Clerks are increasingly working in large open-plan offices, and administrators are coming together in larger groups. Draughtsmen are particularly concentrated since their employment is largely confined to a few departments in fairly large firms. Professionals such as engineers are being employed together in larger numbers.[1]

Similar changes are taking place in the administration of white-collar employees at all levels. For some of them, terms and conditions of employment are still determined on an individual basis with their employer, but the increasing scale of organizations and work groups is leading to greater standardization of conditions. The extreme case is bureaucratic administration. Here, emphasis is on the role rather than its occupant, and positions in the hierarchy and salary levels are rationally assigned by a remote authority. In the private sector of the economy, bureaucracy is typically tempered with administrative particularism, and salary scales, although they exist, are not revealed.

The opportunity for upward promotion has traditionally existed for white-collar employees, and surveys reveal the good promotion prospects for clerks as compared with most blue-collar employees [62]. However, the promotion prospects for many lower white-collar employees are now diminishing. Technical change and bureaucratization are both leading to a more rigid classification of functions, with a clearer distinction between clerical and managerial posts. Often the latter posts are filled directly by the better educated and trained. Nevertheless, a survey finds that 38 per cent of clerks still consider their promotion prospects as fairly good, and only a small percentage consider them poor [63]. Promotion opportunities for bank clerks,[2] draughtsmen [64], and most higher white-collar employees remain fairly good.

The concentration of employees is a measurable factor, and a significant correlation has been found between employment concentration and the density of membership of unions for white-collar employees in manufacturing industry [65]. This

---

[1] In the United States, professional engineers and scientists are coming to be treated as just another part of the labour force. See B. Goldstein, 'Some Aspects of the Nature of Unionism among Salaried Professionals in Industry', *American Sociological Review*, 1955, Vol. 20, pp. 200–1.

[2] One out of two male entrants rise to become managers or executives.

means that differences in the degree of employment concentration differentiate the density of union membership on an occupational and industrial basis.

A more impersonal and bureaucratic administration is typically associated with a higher degree of physical concentration of white-collar employees. Bureaucracy is an important factor leading employees at all levels to join organizations of white-collar unionism [66]. Thus in the Civil Service, which is an example of an almost pure bureaucracy, the density of membership of trade unions and of professional associations is high. The converse case to bureaucracy is administrative particularism, and here there is a lack of standardization in conditions or content of work and a veil of secrecy surrounding pay. This is quite a common situation in private industry, and it partly explains the low density of union membership among white-collar employees here.[1]

The reason why physical concentration in peer groups and bureaucratic administration lead to an increase in the membership of white-collar unionism is that they give rise to feelings of collective interdependence among white-collar employees. They realize that the only effective relationship with their employer must be on a collective basis, and so they join trade unions or professional associations. Furthermore, unionism, when established, leads to further bureaucratization through its demands for even treatment and through the setting up of formal channels of communication. This has been the case in local government, where a bureaucratic administration has been established along with the growth of NALGO [67].

From the viewpoint of unions and professional associations, larger establishments and larger work groups make the recruitment and servicing of members easier. In the converse case, the division of the white-collar labour force into many small establishments, departments and offices can lead to a situation where an employee lacks the opportunity to join a union. This has been observed in banking, where a new clerk may enter a small branch which has no union members [68].

[1] *Supra*, pp. 24–9. The attitudes of employers are also a contributory factor here, see *infra*, pp. 56–61.

The larger the establishment, the more the employer needs a formal system of industrial relations. He may then himself encourage employees to join trade unions or professional associations, or alternatively he may sponsor and support membership of a staff association.

Bureaucracy and physical concentration do not, by themselves, determine whether employees join trade unions rather than staff associations or professional associations. They do, however, have a general indirect influence on the nature of unionism in that, by leading to an increase in membership, they give organizations of unionism the potential of being more effective. This factor, coupled with the opportunity offered by larger firms, leads unions, and professional associations to a lesser extent, to become more active and to engage in interplant bargaining.[1]

The varying types of work that different white-collar employees are engaged in affects their behaviour towards unionism. At a trivial level, only employees in certain occupations are eligible to join professional associations. Among these professionals, as among white-collar employees in general, the more that they are separated from the exercise of authority in their jobs, the more likely are they to join unions. This phenomenon has been particularly observed among technologists and technicians engaged in production [69]. The reason for this is that these employees are made particularly aware of their divorce from the management of the enterprise, and so they join an organization which can represent their interests and give them some control over their work environment.

Another explanation that is sometimes advanced is that white-collar employees in production are in close contact with blue-collar employees and so observe the benefits of union membership. However, no general relationship has been found between social and physical proximity to blue-collar union members and density of union membership among white-collar employees [70]. Nevertheless, contact with blue-collar employees does have some influence on the types of unions that white-collar employees join. In mining, many clerks are

[1] Infra, p. 99.

organized by the NUM, and in printing many of them are organized by NATSOPA, rather than by white-collar unions.

White-collar employees who do a production job, and join an organization of unionism, tend to be more militant than other white-collar employees. This is because they are in a stronger position to win concessions through industrial action. Draughtsmen, for example, can halt production by the withdrawal of their labour, and this is a contributory factor to the militancy of TASS. Engineers and scientists engaged in production are in a similar position, whereas those engaged in research would have little effect on a firm in the short term if they withdrew their labour. The BMA is able actively to pursue its members' interests because they are employed in key positions, and therefore have strong bargaining power.

When managers join unions, these are typically noted for their low militancy. The reason for this stems partly from the managers' sense of responsibility towards their work [71].

Opportunities for promotion are a factor affecting white-collar unionism. However, in so far as some occupations with good promotion prospects exhibit high membership density of unionism, e.g. local government, banking, while some exhibit low membership density, e.g. professional engineers; and some occupations with poor promotion prospects exhibit high membership density of unionism, e.g. railway clerks, while some exhibit low membership density, e.g. shop assistants; the factor is not a fundamental determinant of the membership of white-collar unionism. Other factors distinguish industrial and occupational differences in membership.

Other things being equal, the better any white-collar group perceive their promotion opportunities to be, the less likely are they to join a union. Rather they will seek individual betterment, or they may perhaps join a professional association in order to obtain a qualification which will be of use in personal advancement [72]. Where promotion prospects exist, but other factors favour the growth of unionism, white-collar employees are likely to form a vertical union, e.g. NALGO, NUBE. This, typically, will exhibit low militancy, partly because it contains a hierarchy of grades and therefore lacks a common unifying purpose, and partly because employees fear that participation in militant action might damage their chances of gaining promotion [73].

When white-collar employees perceive that for one reason or another they cannot gain expected promotion, then they are likely to join organizations of white-collar unionism.) Thus clerks at a steelworks joined a union largely as a result of blocked promotion arising from the introduction of a management trainee scheme [74]. The reason for this is that blocked promotion increases group cohesion, and gives employees a stimulus for winning improved terms for all their group. Such organizations are likely to be fairly militant since they have a unified purpose. For example, a survey carried out in 1968 found that male teachers who were not going to get headships viewed militancy in a more favourable light than did other groups of teachers [75].

The trend for the future is towards larger organizations, more impersonal administration, and an increasing demand for paper qualifications as entry requirements to various occupations. All these factors will increase the membership density of white-collar unionism, and, to the extent that promotion is blocked, may also contribute to increasing militancy.[1]

ATTITUDE OF EMPLOYERS

The attitudes of employers towards white-collar unionism and the actions in which these attitudes result have a considerable influence on the behaviour of white-collar employees.

In the public sector of the economy, the pluralistic nature of the industrial organization is accepted, and there is a favourable attitude towards white-collar unionism [76]. Along with the realization that industry can never be administered solely in the interests of the employees, and therefore that conflict is in-

[1] In Australia many unions organizing white-collar employees are behaving in the same way as the blue-collar unions. See R. M. Martin, 'Australian Professional and White-Collar Unions', Symposium, *Industrial Relations*, October 1965, p. 98.

herent in an industrial organization, comes the welcoming of trade unions and other independent organizations which recognize the conflict in that '. . . they at least make it possible for this conflict to be contained, controlled and eventually resolved' [77]. Thus the Civil Service, nationalized industries, the National Health Service, and local government, not only recognize independent organizations for white-collar employees, but also encourage their staffs to join [78].

In the private sector of the economy many employers still see an industrial organization as a unitary system, having one source of authority and one focus of loyalty. They adopt this frame of reference partly to legitimize their power [79]. As a consequence, such employers never completely accept unions or other organizations which present a challenge to their authority. This feeling is particularly strong in connection with their white-collar employees, with whom such employers claim a special relationship. They feel that trade union membership for white-collar employees is unnecessary and they fear the 'dire consequences' of such membership. Chief amongst their fears are that union membership will challenge managerial prerogative, provoke a conflict of loyalty for individuals, particularly managers and supervisors, and that it will stifle ambition and promote general mediocrity [80].

These hostile attitudes towards white-collar membership of trade unions manifest themselves in several ways. One of these has been the refusal of recognition, and in 1964, 27 per cent of the total labour force was located in areas in which employers generally refused to recognize trade unions. This included the distributive trades and much of manufacturing industry for white-collar employees. Another 11 per cent were in areas with a partial recognition problem, e.g. white-collar employees in the construction industry. A further 7·4 per cent of the labour force was in areas where trade unions have not yet tried to organize, but which are almost certain to present recognition problems in the future, e.g. most professional and scientific services and white-collar employees in textiles, leather and furniture [81]. The DE has estimated that some 85 per cent of white-collar employees in manufacturing industries are not covered by collective agreements [82]. A survey carried out by the old British Employers' Confederation confirms this general picture [83]. In fact engineering and newspaper publishing are the only private industries where unions for white-collar employees are generally recognized. There is, however, a slight trend towards increasing recognition of these unions [84].

Two common reasons have usually been advanced by employers for refusing recognition to a union. One of these is that a particular union is not the appropriate one to represent a particular grade of employees in a particular industry [85]. For example, the British Federation of Master Printers has refused to recognize NATSOPA for clerical workers and prefers to recognize APECCS [86], and Stewart and Lloyds Ltd, Corby, has refused to recognize ASTMS for supervisors and instead prefers ISTC [87]. NUBE has had a long struggle for recognition from the clearing banks [88]. The other objection commonly raised by employers is that a particular union is not representative of the grades that it seeks to represent. On this factor, as on the previous one, the employer can choose any criteria that he likes in order to justify non-recognition. For example, in shipbuilding APECCS has been refused recognition even in establishments where it has a high degree of organization because the Shipbuilding Employers' Federation has demanded a substantial proportion of membership throughout the industry as a whole [89].

Even when recognition is conceded by employers, this may be limited to informal discussion of individual members' grievances and exclude full negotiating rights for the union [90]. One such example is the recognition conceded by the British Spinners' and Doublers' Association to the Textile Officials' Association [91].

A second strategy that hostile employers use to prevent the growth of union membership among their white-collar employees may be dubbed peaceful competition. This includes fostering administrative particularism, paying generous salaries and fringe benefits, and establishing staff associations [92]. The latter are easily dominated and can be awarded concessions only to the extent that the employer considers necessary (see below, pp. 106–7) [93]. An extension of this tactic is to sponsor other bodies to discourage union membership; a famous example was the Foreman and Staff Mutual Benefit Society which used to have a rule stating that it was not possible to belong both to it and to a trade union, so that by joining the latter a member forfeited his claim to benefits [94].

Some employers have resorted to forcible opposition to union membership by white-collar employees. They may discriminate against union members in pay and promotion, and even dismiss prominent members [95]. Some specific examples of discrimination have been found [96].

There is some evidence that the attitude of employers is a discriminating factor explaining differences in the density of union membership among white-collar employees. Thus in the public sector, where the attitude is generally favourable, union membership is fairly high, whereas in the private sector it is fairly low. Within the private sector, density of union membership among white-collar employees is highest in the engineering and newspaper publishing industries, where, as mentioned (pp. 27–8), some form of recognition has existed for several years [97].

There are several reasons for this. One is that many white-collar employees, and women in particular, do not wish to offend their employer, and so will not join a union against his wish. Further, many white-collar employees in the private sector fear discrimination, and this is particularly acute for those whose skills are peculiar to their own firm and relatively worthless outside it, since they are in a very vulnerable position. Another reason is that some employers deliberately foster an atmosphere which is not conducive to the growth of union membership, and in particular they attempt to avoid an overtly bureaucratic administration.

The most important way in which the attitude of employers affects the density of union membership is through the factor of recognition, however. Without being recognized a union cannot be effective and therefore white-collar employees see no instrumental advantages in joining. Hence 20 per cent of bank clerks gave non-recognition as their reason for not joining

NUBE [98]. A vicious circle is set up since low membership in itself precludes recognition.

The attitude of employers in general, and the factor of recognition in particular, has some indirect effects on the nature of unions for white-collar employees. To be effective in a hostile environment the union must be fairly militant, but it is in this environment that factors act to keep membership low and the union consequently weak. However, there is some evidence that militancy in a hostile environment pays, and that strike action is the most successful method of securing recognition [99]. The converse is not necessarily true, and the behaviour of unions in a situation where they are recognized by the employer depends on a variety of factors.[1]

The membership of staff associations increases where the employer has an unfavourable attitude towards unions, since in this situation staff associations are sponsored. In the public sector staff associations are not found at all.

The attitude of employers has little effect on the membership of professional associations. These are not typically opposed by employers in the private sector since the ideology of professional associations generally accepts no conflict between themselves and the employer.[2]

In the public sector, to the extent that the membership of trade unions is encouraged the membership of professional associations might be thought to be suppressed. This is not, however, the case, since in this environment professional associations shift their nature somewhat and become recognized as bargaining agents for certain groups of employees.[3]

The Industrial Relations Act 1971 will not by itself alter the attitude of employers towards white-collar unionism. However, by making it an unfair industrial practice for an employer to discriminate against an employee because he is a member of a registered union, and by providing a mechanism to enable representative unions to gain recognition, the Act will remove a factor which is artificially depressing the membership of unions,

[1] Supra, pp. 30–56.
[2] Supra, p. 32.
[3] Infra, pp. 111–21.

and could lead to a great increase in membership.[1] At the same time membership of staff associations could fall unless they drastically change in nature.[2] The extent to which this will happen will depend on unions' attitudes to the Act in general and to registration in particular.[3] Professional associations in the private sector of the economy will increasingly act like those in the public sector.

GOVERNMENT INFLUENCE AND LEGISLATION

Until very recently the system of industrial relations in Britain has favoured a minimum of state influence and regulation [100]. Nevertheless the framework of labour law [101], however scanty it has been, together with government social and economic policy, has exerted an influence on white-collar unionism.

It is in the area of trade union recognition that government action has had the most direct effects. Historical evidence shows that in the periods during and after World War I, when the Whitley Committee recommended the establishment of Joint Industrial Councils, and around World War II, when the National Arbitration Tribunal was established by Order 1305, some recognition of trade unions for white-collar employees came about in private industry [102]. Even in the public sector it was only the provision for unilateral arbitration that enabled NALGO to persuade all local authorities to grant recognition and negotiating rights [103]. Since the end of World War II, the replacement of Order 1305 by Order 1376 in 1951, and the replacement of this by the Terms and Conditions of Employment Act 1959, have made it successively more difficult for unions to use statutory provisions to gain recognition, and little further recognition has been won in private industry. Thus the evidence is that most recognition of unions for white-collar employees in private industry has come about, directly or indirectly, as a result of government policies [104].

[1] Infra, pp. 63–4.
[2] Infra, pp. 106–8.
[3] Infra, pp. 83–6.

Allied with the question of recognition is that of the right of trade union membership. The position before the Industrial Relations Act 1971 was that although Britain had ratified two International Labour Conventions – Nos 87 and 98 – dealing with the rights of employees to join organizations of their own choice and the protection of employees against acts of anti-trade union discrimination, there was nothing in the law, outside of the nationalized industries, to prevent employers from deliberately obstructing freedom of association.

The effects of this position on union recognition and rights of membership has been to suppress union membership in those parts of the private sector where employers have an unfavourable attitude towards trade unions. At the same time, membership of staff associations has been enhanced.[1]

In the public sector, the government encourages its own employees to belong to appropriate unions, and the boards of nationalized industries have a statutory obligation to grant trade union recognition. This leads to high union membership.[1] Government contractors are obliged to recognize the freedom of their employees to belong to unions, but there has been no requirement to recognize the unions for negotiation. Since recognition is the key factor for increase in the density of union membership, the policy has had little effect on union membership.

However, changes have taken place in the government attitude to trade union membership and recognition. The Royal Commission on Trade Unions and Employers' Associations 1965–8 (the Donovan Commission) supported the idea of collective bargaining for white-collar employees, and saw that the growth of this was largely dependent upon recognition by employers [105]. Towards this end, they recommended that any stipulation in a contract of employment that an employee is not to belong to a union should in law be void [106]. They recommended that employers should recognize unions unless the employer can show that his employees are unwilling to join. The Commission on Industrial Relations, which was established by the Labour Government following the recommendation of the

[1] Supra, pp. 56–61.

Donovan Commission, had as one of its original duties the investigation of cases of non-recognition, and the Donovan Commission recommended the restoration of unilateral arbitration to back up the CIR's recommendations. They also recommended the setting up of safeguards for employees against unfair dismissal. One example cited was dismissal as a result of being a union member [107]. These recommendations would have been implemented in full by the then Labour Government [108].

The return of a Conservative Government in June 1970 led to the tabling of a bill which became law as the Industrial Relations Act 1971. This gives employees a right to belong to a registered union of their choice and to take part in its activities, and an equal right, except where an agency shop agreement or an approved closed shop agreement is in force, not to belong to a union. Discrimination by an employer against an employee exercising these rights is an unfair industrial practice and the employee has the right of complaint to an industrial tribunal [109]. The Act also establishes procedures for the resolution of disputes over trade union recognition and bargaining rights through the use of the new National Industrial Relations Court and the CIR [110]. (In general the legislation has many similarities to that existing in the United States [111].)

This legislation provides unions with an opportunity to increase their membership in the private sector through gaining recognition. The extent to which they are able to do this will depend on the extent to which they appear attractive and effective to white-collar employees and the extent to which they are prepared to use the provisions in the Act.[1] At the same time, unions may well become more militant in that high membership makes militancy possible and effective, and there is some evidence that militant activity attracts membership.[2] This will not be universal, however, and will depend on a variety of circumstances, including other provisions in the Act.[3] (The legislation will mark a change in the position of staff associations,

[1] Infra, pp. 101–3.
[2] Supra, p. 34.
[3] Infra, pp. 101–3.

leading to the decline of some and the growth of others.[1] To the extent that trade unions are seen to be effective, the Act may result in a decrease in the membership of some professional associations, or alternatively professional associations may modify their nature so that they can be equally attractive to prospective members.[2]

The Government is becoming increasingly involved in many other aspects of the employment situation. The Contracts of Employment Act 1963, the Redundancy Payments Act 1965, and the National Insurance Act 1966, are examples of legislation which lay down minimum conditions for all employees. This is having a two-sided influence on white-collar unionism.

On one hand the legislation is a factor acting to narrow the gap in conditions of employment between blue-collar and white-collar employees, and in so doing it is in sympathy with the Donovan Commission and the general policy of the last Government [112]. As such it is a spur to the membership and activity of white-collar unionism, as these employees wish to obtain superior conditions to blue-collar employees.[3] On the other hand legislation provides minimum safeguards at least, for all white-collar employees, and so may make some of them feel less need to join an organization of unionism.

The general economic policies of government have an indirect effect on white-collar unionism since they influence the level of employment and the rate of inflation.

In fact all legislation which has a direct or indirect effect on the general situation of white-collar employees serves to indicate to them the increasing government influence in this field. It makes white-collar employees increasingly aware that in order to exert an effective influence over their environment they need to combine together in organizations which can make representations on these matters. Thus legislation, by itself, is leading to an increase in the membership of white-collar unionism, and in particular trade unions since these have channels of communication with the government. Incomes

[1] Infra, pp. 105–8.
[2] Infra, pp. 111–15.
[3] Supra, pp. 47–51.

policy was strongly opposed, particularly by white-collar unions in the public sector where the policy was most vigorously applied, and union pressure led to the collapse of this policy. Similarly, union pressure led to the abandonment of the 'penal clauses' proposed by the Labour Government in *In Place of Strife* [113]. These successes are in themselves instrumental in making more white-collar employees join unions, and in making unions increasingly militant. The unions failed to prevent the passing of the Industrial Relations Act 1971, but some of them, at least, are united in their boycott of its operation.

4 · *Characteristics of White-Collar Unionism*

Structural Pattern

The structural pattern of trade unions has traditionally been described in terms of craft unions, occupational unions, industrial unions and general unions; or alternatively in terms of horizontal and vertical unions [1]. These terms are inadequate to describe the hybrid forms existing and evolving, and so the concept of open and closed unions is valuable [2].

An open union may recruit all types of employees, while a closed union will limit sharply and definitely its area of recruitment. Unions adopt a form which appears to them to best serve their interests, and the relative openness or closedness of a union can alter quite dramatically as leadership and members respond to a changing industrial and occupational balance.

Open unions typically show the largest growth in membership as a result of recruitment and amalgamation. NALGO, for example, sees its area of concern as the whole public sector apart from the Civil Service, and all public utilities except the railways. ASSET amalgamated with AScW to form ASTMS, and this union continues to grow not only through the vigorous recruitment of scientific and technical workers and managers, but also through further amalgamations with, for example, the Prudential Staff Associations and other organizations of insurance workers, and the MPU. Closed unions do, however, sometimes amalgamate, as illustrated by the example of NGA which brings together certain 'craft' grades within the printing industry [3].

Amalgamation into larger units gives unions the advantages

of being able to formulate and implement more comprehensive policies, to exert a greater influence at industrial and national levels, to provide more services for their members, and probably to eliminate the uneconomic duplication of officials. Thus, from 1964 to 1968, 53 unions were involved in amalgamations [4]. Not all amalgamations are successful, however, as illustrated by the split in SOGAT in 1970.

Openness and closedness both result in there being white-collar unions and partially white-collar unions. ASTMS and NALGO have shown their openness in forming larger white-collar unions. DATA has shown its increasing openness by firstly expanding its scope of membership to include allied technicians in the engineering industry, and secondly by amalgamating with AUEW (when it became known as TASS) to form a large partially white-collar union. TGWU has become a partially white-collar union through its openness in recruiting more clerks, supervisors and technicians.

CPSA has remained a white-collar union through its relatively closed formula of confining its recruitment to clerical grades in the Civil Service.[1] ISTC follows the closed formula of industrial unionism, and as such forms a partially white-collar union. POEU is a fairly closed union which is changing into a partially white-collar union as technical change in its industry transfers jobs from craftsmen and unskilled employees to technicians.

The type of union that white-collar employees form or join depends on the circumstances. Where skills are largely confined to one industry, and career progression is typically within the industry, then a union containing a vertical structure is often formed, giving advantages of continuity of membership and comprehensive and integrated policies. Examples include NALGO and AUEW–TASS. Where common interests and career development are seen on an occupational plane, then unions with a broadly horizontal structure are usually found, e.g. APECCS and ASTMS.

White-collar employees often see their 'immediate' interests –

[1] There are signs that CPSA is now becoming more open, e.g. it is seeking to retain membership in the Post Office Corporation.

i.e. short-term economic interests, and their 'ideological' interests – i.e. wider political interests, as differing from those of blue-collar employees, even though their 'instrumental' interests – i.e. issues such as the legal status of trade unions, may be the same [5]. For this reason they join or form white-collar unions, and sometimes these take quite a hostile attitude towards blue-collar unions [6]. Those white-collar employees who do join partially white-collar unions are generally people who have been promoted from blue-collar grades, or whose social origins or conditions of work are similar to those of blue-collar employees, and who therefore have sympathy with them. This is so, for example, in NUR and EETU–PTU [7].

Within the white-collar group there are sectional interests, and higher grade employees often form their own separate unions. Examples include BTOG in transport and BACM in coal mining; while within NALGO, the Society of Town Clerks and the Association of Local Government Finance Officers are virtually autonomous for negotiating purposes [8].

Over the years, the growth trends of unions have led to a reduction in their overall number, but no reduction in multiplicity or overlapping [9]. Within any one company there may be different unions for each of the main occupational groups, and, further, there may be more than one union competing for membership within a given group of employees. An example is found in local government where there is some overlap between NUPE, CHSE, FBU, HVA, TGWU and GMWU.

The disadvantages of this situation include the complication of collective bargaining and grievance procedures, problems of co-ordinating policies, and difficulties over recruitment and servicing of members [10]. It can lead to inter-union disputes over demarcation or recognition. For example, clashes between TASS and ASTMS over the organization and representation of the same group of workers led to the disputes at C. A. Parsons, Newcastle, and Standard Telephones and Cables, Monkstown, in 1970. In the public sector, there were clashes between APECCS and ISTC in 1969 over the representation of clerical workers.

One solution frequently canvassed for this structural problem is industrial unionism. The claimed advantages for this include the harmonization of sectional claims on behalf of different occupational groups within a workplace; simpler negotiation, consultation and grievance procedures; simplification of demarcation problems; elimination of inter-union competition; the simplification of the internal structure of unions, with branches based on the workplace; and the making of planning at national level easier. However, industrial unionism does have disadvantages. The boundaries of industries are seldom clear and distinct, and technical change alters them. Many companies engage in activities spanning several industries and these may be accommodated on the same site, while many employees see their main interests occupationally rather than industrially. The decisive objection to industrial unionism is the practical one, since the natural growth pattern of unions is towards the formation of open unions operating in broad sectors. There are, in fact, no real examples of industrial unions in Britain, and although ISTC and CHSE, for example, aspire towards this form, there are other unions also operating in these industries.

The Donovan Commission made several recommendations having a bearing on the structural pattern of trade unions. One of these was that the existing structural pattern could be rationalized by unions accepting the principle of one union for one grade of work within one factory. There would be provision for third-party arbitration, probably through the TUC, where more than one union already had members [11]. Another was that official inter-union committees should be established by the unions to alleviate the effects of multi-unionism [12]. A third recommendation proposed that companies should draw up and register their own collective agreements with the DE [13].

This last recommendation was accepted by the previous Government [14]. Had it been implemented, its long-term effects would have been to lead to much closer co-operation between unions within a company, and even to the formation of a single union for all grades within a company. The last Government also proposed a scheme to provide loans and grants to assist in the amalgamation of unions or the transfer of engagements between unions [15]. However, its defeat in the

1970 General Election meant that this potentially powerful aid for assisting in the reform of trade union structure was never implemented.

The legislation of the present Government takes no direct steps to reform the structural pattern of trade unions. The establishment of a joint negotiating panel as the sole bargaining agent in a bargaining unit may possibly serve to increase inter-union co-operation [16]. However, there is an opposite, and probably valid, viewpoint that deplores the temporary nature of the recognized sole bargaining agent and believes that it will in fact result in the growth of breakaway unions.[1] If this did take place, it would aggravate the existing structural problem. An example is the London Fire Fighters' Federation which has broken away from the FBU and is now seeking to register. One other aspect of the Act which will influence an effect, but not a cause, of the structural pattern of unions, is the proposal to make recognition strikes an unfair industrial practice [17]. The financial penalties provided for in the Act will provide a big disincentive to recognition strikes taking place [18].

Although it seems that external agencies will do little in the near future to help rationalize union structure, the movement itself is taking steps in this direction. Individual unions are increasingly adopting internal structures which follow more closely the occupational or industrial interests of their members.[2] At the same time the TUC is co-operating with unions in trying to co-ordinate their activities and prevent inter-union disputes. It has proposed that it should set up, in conjunction with the unions concerned, a system of industrial committees to examine areas such as recruitment, inter-union relations, collective bargaining, industrial and trade union training, wage structures, and safety and health [19]. This move is in sympathy with the recommendations of the Donovan Commission. The Steel Industry Trade Union Consultative Committee is a step in this direction, and transport, local government, engineer-

---

[1] Twenty per cent of the employees in a bargaining unit may apply to the National Industrial Relations Court for a change in the sole bargaining agent. See *Industrial Relations Act 1971*, ss. 51–3.

[2] Infra, pp. 71–6.

ing and the health services are areas suggested for new committees.

Internal Organization

The internal organization adopted by any individual union organizing white-collar employees is the product of a number of interrelated factors. One influence is the historical development of the union. This will have determined not only its membership size and distribution on a geographical, industrial and occupational basis, but also the extent to which groups have separate representation as a result of their being brought into the union through amalgamations. Another influence is the organization of employers and employers' associations and the resultant pattern of collective bargaining existing within the union's sphere of interest. A third influence is the policies of the union itself, and in particular its plans for future growth and how it views its bargaining role for various groups. The internal organizations of different unions are, therefore, to varying degrees, a statement of their historical origins and a conscious adaptation to their present and projected situations.

NALGO has over 1,400 branches, and these are based on the geographical areas where members work. Generally there are separate branches for each group of employees organized, e.g. local government, gas, electricity, health service. Above the branches are 12 districts, and each branch can send at least one delegate to serve on the district council. There are additionally at district level several service conditions committees for each sector organized. Each branch of NALGO sends at least one delegate to the annual conference, which decides national policy. There are also 'Group Annual Meetings' of representatives from the various sectors. The national executive council, which is made up of district representatives, exists to see that the policies are carried out, and it appoints all full-time officers.

The basic unit of organization in TASS is the office, which has an elected committee, and offices are grouped into branches which are based on members' workplaces. Above these are 14 divisional councils. The supreme decision-making body is the annual conference, and the executive committee implements these decisions. The executive committee is advised of the particular interests of members employed in the shipbuilding, aircraft, and nationalized industries by a system of advisory panels elected by and from members in those areas. TASS has a close relationship with STCS, and each is represented on the executive committee of the other.

APECCS has a system of branches based on a single firm or containing members employed in only one industry, and above these area councils and the executive council. There are additionally a number of advisory councils which function at both regional and national level. They cover industries where the union has membership, e.g. engineering, coal, electricity supply, and advise the area councils and the executive council on matters within each industry. APECCS also convenes *ad hoc* meetings of members employed in combines.

The smallest organizational unit of ASTMS[1] is the group, which is based on a particular factory. Above these are the branches which organize separately the differing grades in each geographical area. The union feels that having separate technical and supervisory branches, executive branches, etc. removes any conflict of interest for members that might otherwise occur. Above the branches are the 11 district councils, the annual delegate conference which decides policy, and the national executive council which implements it.

ASTMS is becoming increasingly aware of the diminishing usefulness of district boundaries for matters other than administration, and is moulding its organization to follow companies and industries. It has instigated 'combine conferences' for delegates from all plants of a company, and has established national industrial councils in areas such as civil air transport, where its membership is covered by national negotiating machinery.

NUBE has a fairly traditional structure of branches, each of which sends delegates to the area council, which in turn elects members to the national executive committee. Each branch sends a delegate to the annual delegate meeting, which is the

[1] Here I concentrate on Division A, the rules of ASSET. Division 1, AScW, has rules broadly similar to APECCS.

governing body of the union. There is a feeling that this structure is inadequate, and reorganization into 11 regions is being considered.

Partially white-collar unions can be distinguished by the extent to which they make special provisions for their white-collar members. EETU–PTU has a separate technical and supervisory section, which means that most of its white-collar members are in either special branches or special sections of a general branch. In the event of any disputes, members of the technical and supervisory section come under the direct control of the national executive council. The union has abolished area committees, and instead links branches with industrial conferences at national and area levels. NATSOPA [20] has rather similar arrangements for the separate representation of its white-collar members.

TGWU has a trade group structure, one of which (ACTSS) caters for white-collar members. This has its own branches, above which are regional trade group committees which elect a national trade group committee. It has its own full-time officers. The trade groups are linked together through the biennial delegate conference, the supreme policy-making authority of TGWU, which is constituted from branches and regional trade groups, and the general executive council, which is made up of representatives from national trade group committees and geographical regions of the union.

GMWU has traditionally had an organization consisting of a mixture of general branches and specialized industrial branches, and over these district councils, a general council, and an annual congress. However, this structure is now being altered to provide factory-based or industrial branches, and where numbers permit, separate provisions for white-collar members. Along with this there will be the building up of industrial groupings, one of which will be a clerical group, with district and national industrial conferences, but these will only be advisory bodies. The national executive committees, general council and congress will remain as the main organs of government.

In NUM the clerical and junior administrative staff and the

supervisory staff each have their own branches, and these are administratively grouped together in one 'area' of the union, namely the colliery officials' and staffs' area. This area has direct negotiations with the National Coal Board at the various levels. The position is similar in NUR.

POEU does not have separate branches for its white-collar members, but meets their needs along with other occupational groups by having the executive composed to represent different interests, and using occupational committees for much of executive work, and by dividing the annual conference into occupational conferences on some issues. UPW makes similar arrangements.

NUPE has some separate branches for white-collar employees, but at district and national level divisions are on a service basis, while election to the executive council is on a geographical basis. CHSE has no special arrangements within its rules for white-collar members.

ISTC has separate branches for white-collar employees, with their own annual conference, and there are a proportion of seats on the executive council reserved for the clerical, administrative, technical and supervisory staff section.

Any attempt to compare the effectiveness of the internal organizations of various unions organizing white-collar employees is fraught with difficulties. There are problems of the choice of criteria of effectiveness, and of measurement on these criteria.

One possible method would be to start from the viewpoint of the members, and find which unions have shown the greatest growth in membership over recent years. The overriding objection to this is that so many factors other than internal organization influence the growth of unions.[1] Nevertheless GMWU took their relatively static total membership as one reason for reorganizing their structure [21]. An alternative approach would be to carry out a survey among members of various unions to see which kind of internal organization they prefer. The likely findings would be that employees would have different preferences depending on their circumstances. In fact

[1] Supra, Chapter 3.

there is no evidence that white-collar employees as a whole prefer any particular type of union internal structure [22].

A second possible method would be to look at unions and try to discover how successful they have been in furthering their members' interests. The objection to this as a measure of the effectiveness of the internal organization of various unions is that so many other factors internal and external to a union influence its success. A third possible measure of a union's success, that of developing criteria for unions such as the number of full-time officers needed to service a given number of employees to a defined standard, is really a non-starter. Unions are rated by their external impact, and not by their internal administrative efficiency.

It is important to realize that all the characteristics of the internal organization of unions which some members, at least, would rate as desirable, are not mutually attainable. One example of this is that the greater the arrangements made for the special representation of the specific interests of groups within the union, the more fragmented the union becomes, and with a reduction in its unity comes a reduction in its bargaining power. This problem is particularly acute for partially white-collar unions.

The extent to which an informal structure, typified by shop stewards, grows up within a union is to some extent a measure of the appropriateness of its internal organization to the task that it is trying to do. Shop stewards do not play a very prominent role in most unions catering for white-collar employees, though it does not follow from this that their organizations are necessarily superior to those of some blue-collar unions. The main reasons for the relative absence of shop stewards is that factors such as the decentralization of decision-making and the presence of incentive payment schemes and overtime earnings, which encourage the growth of a strong shop-steward movement, are largely absent from white-collar employment. Even in unions like the AUEW, where there is a strong shop-steward movement among the blue-collar members, arrangements are made so that shop stewards do not negotiate for white-collar members.

In ASTMS, the grade representative is in many ways similar to a shop steward, and negotiates with local management on matters which only concern his group of members. However, grade representatives have detailed directives on how they should work [23]. They are therefore integrated into the formal internal organization of the union, and so do not present a threat to it.

Two trends in internal organization which are likely to continue into the future are a concentration of union branches on the workplace and a provision of separate representation for special interest groups. The former is in sympathy with the conduct of industrial relations at factory level and with an increase in membership participation, and the latter is both a cause and effect of amalgamations between unions.[1]

Membership Participation

One way in which the extent of membership participation can be measured is by the numbers taking part in the formal processes of union government. On this measure many white-collar unions achieve higher membership participation than most blue-collar unions. For example, the NUT achieves 21 per cent average attendance at ordinary branch meetings and 25 per cent at annual general meetings, compared with blue-collar unions which show an attendance at branch meetings of between 3 and 15 per cent, with the concentration at the lower end of the range. In union elections white-collar unions also typically show fairly high membership participation: NUT achieves a 46 per cent poll for the national executive and in NALGO over 50 per cent vote in branch elections. There are exceptions to this general picture: CPSA averages 5 per cent attendance at branch meetings and TSSA averages 5 to 7 per cent attendance, although the latter union shows a 64 per cent average poll in elections [24].

Although no separate figures are available for the attendance at meetings or participation in polls of white-collar employees in partially white-collar unions, there are other indicators of their participation in the formal union government. In some of

[1] Supra, pp. 66–9, and infra, pp. 76–80.

these unions white-collar employees have more than their proportional representation on various bodies. For example, in 1964-5 the white-collar membership of TGWU, as accounted for by ACTSS, made up 4 per cent of the total membership of the union, while 4·9 per cent of the membership of the regional committees of the union and 4·6 per cent of the delegates at the union delegate conference came from ACTSS [25]. In other unions the reverse position holds, and ISTC, for example, up to the mid 1960s had only ever had one white-collar member appointed to a full-time position within the union [26].

The extent of participation in unions by members is largely influenced by the size, structure and government of the unions, and the fact that white-collar members often show higher participation than blue-collar members derives mainly from differences in these factors.

The larger the union, the more diverse the membership is likely to be, and the more difficult it is to give representation to specific interest groups and to link them directly to the central policy-making machinery. Thus large unions have a tendency for low membership participation. However, many white-collar unions are fairly small, while in some of the larger ones there is some decentralization of decision-making, as in ASTMS, or the retention of the direct link between branches and the annual conference, as in NALGO. Many partially white-collar unions make special provisions for the representation of their white-collar members.[1] There is evidence that small branches based on the workplace encourage high participation since they encourage interpersonal contact, give a sense of involvement, and cut out the problem of travelling long distances to meetings [27].

The size of a union, and related to this its tendency towards openness or closedness, influence its style of government. H. A. Turner distinguished three styles of union government, an 'exclusive democracy', an 'aristocracy', and a 'popular bossdom' [28]. The first style of government is found in unions with a predominantly closed character, and it encourages high membership participation. A white-collar example is ACTT. In the second type, one section of the membership plays a

[1] Supra, pp. 73-4.

dominant role and exhibits high participation. For example, the draughtsmen in TASS and the senior grades in NALGO exert a disproportionate influence in those unions. A 'popular bossdom' type of union is predominantly open, and concentrates initiative in the hands of full-time officials, and so exhibits low membership participation in general. Many partially white-collar unions, e.g. NUPE, USDAW, can be placed in this category, but white-collar members are likely to show higher participation than the blue-collar members in these unions. This is because white-collar employees join unions owing to particular circumstances in order to obtain certain benefits; they do not join just by convention.[1] They are therefore unlikely to join the ranks of the apathetic. Furthermore, factors such as high labour turnover which lead to low participation are largely confined to lower skilled employees (in USDAW, for example, 100,000 members lapse annually [29]), and so, with the exception of shop assistants, do not apply to any great extent to white-collar employees in partially white-collar unions.

The systems that unions use to appoint their executives and full-time officers affect the chances for participation open to members. Those unions that use direct election of full-time officers, e.g. NUM, NUR, give ordinary members a greater opportunity to participate than those in which all full-time officers are selected by the executive, e.g. NUPE, NALGO [30]. In this respect many white-collar unions offer their members reduced opportunities for participation. The election methods used also affect participation. Locating the voting process in branches which are divorced from the place of work or using a system of branch block voting, both discourage membership participation. These methods are found in some partially white-collar unions, e.g. USDAW, GMWU, but are largely absent from white-collar unions [31]. The use, as in NUT and other white-collar unions, of a system of postal voting, with the collector urging and reminding members to vote, encourages high membership participation [32].

Some unions take positive steps to encourage participation.

[1] Supra, Chapter 3.

Many white-collar unions send their journals direct to every member, e.g. TASS, NUBE, ASTMS, and this serves to give members information and to encourage their interest in issues.

Participation in the formal channels of union government is not the only measure of membership involvement. Unofficial action at shop-floor level shows the members' wish to exert an influence over their employment situation. This action, however, is largely confined to certain groups of blue-collar employees where a strong shop-steward movement gives it leadership. Its absence among white-collar employees may be attributed to their better understanding of, and ability to use, the formal structure of the union, and their ability to shape this to their needs.

The significance of membership participation in union government has been well documented [33]. A union is by intention a democratic body formed to serve the interests of its members. However, unions must walk on a tight-rope of democracy between, on one side, anarchy, excessive parochialism and short-term perspectives; and on the other side, control by the central government of the union, which impresses its viewpoint on unwilling sections of the membership. Increasingly in unions, as in society in general, an expectation of control by the membership is growing up, and if unions are going to survive in their present form they will have to channel this energy to serve the long-term interests of all their constituent groups. TASS has gone some way towards this by having some 15 per cent of its membership actively engaged as office holders at various levels [34].

In this light it is interesting to examine the likely effects of the Industrial Relations Act 1971. The requirements that unions must hold secret ballots and that members be protected from discrimination will, to a very marginal extent, act to increase membership participation in a few unions where such safeguards do not already exist [35]. The proposal that collective agreements be legally enforceable unless otherwise stated could add a new dimension to membership participation [36]. If legally enforceable agreements are negotiated, and the signs are that neither employers nor unions are eager to do this, then in one sense they would act to increase participation by putting pressure on the union government to negotiate contracts which satisfy the rank and file members. This is because breaking of these contracts by dissatisfied members may lead to levying of fines on either the union or the unofficial leaders [37]. However, the effect of the levying of fines would be to lead to fragmentation of the union and to a weakening of the moral strength of the leadership. Thus the proposals for legally enforceable contracts could also insert a tension into the relations between the leadership and the members of unions, and in this sense would be harmful to membership participation.

Union Officers

In Britain there is on average one full-time union officer for every 3,800 trade union members. There are wide variations between unions, however. For example, in USDAW there is one officer for every 1,978 members and in NALGO there is one officer for every 4,509 members [38].

Full-time officers occupy such posts as general secretary, regional secretary, district secretary, and industrial officer, and in some unions membership of the national executive and the union presidency are full-time posts. The spheres of responsibility of full-time officers vary according to their position in the union hierarchy and the pattern of organization of their unions. For example, in APECCS full-time officers have responsibility for industries or sections of industries, and ASTMS has appointed officers to specialize in companies or industries. Each trade group in TGWU has its own full-time national secretary as well as officers at regional level.

The work of most full-time union officers involves conducting negotiations with employers, interpreting agreements, and investigating breaches of agreements. In this work the officers are acting to serve the interests of their members. Nevertheless, at senior levels in particular, the range of knowledge and experience of the full-time officer puts him in a very powerful position, so that he may, in fact, be largely influencing the expectations and demands of his members and the character of negotiations with employers. This applies particularly to a general secretary, whose personal character and viewpoint may influence the whole character of the union.)One exception to this general picture was NALGO, in which the general secretary used only to be an administrator. However, since 1966 the trend has been for him to become a leader and a spokesman for the union.

The traditional source of union officers has been, and largely remains, the body of the union. This has the advantage of ensuring that officers have an intimate knowledge and experience of the work and the problems of the ordinary union membership, particularly since such officers have typically held voluntary posts within the union for some time. Their social background is typical of the union membership as a whole. However, in partially white-collar unions, better educational opportunities, largely as a result of the Education Act 1944, mean that the supply of potential union officers from low-grade blue-collar jobs is largely drying up. The result of this is that the white-collar members of partially white-collar unions are providing a disproportionately large number of their officers, averaging 26 per cent over the general unions [39]. A further source of officers is from the clerical staff of unions.

Although white-collar unions are not experiencing the same difficulties in finding suitable internal candidates for full-time posts, there is nevertheless a developing trend among them towards recruiting officers externally. This is also found in some partially white-collar unions, e.g. NUPE, POEU. The justification for this is that union officers require a wide range of specialist knowledge on subjects such as economics, sociology, accountancy and law, and that this breadth of knowledge may compensate for a possible lack of personal experience of the industry. Nevertheless there still remains the opinion that '. . . full-time trade union jobs demand more than a mere interest in the work. Officials must be alive with the spirit of the movement . . .' [40]. ASTMS stresses this point in appointing candidates as trainee officers [41]. Those unions that appoint external candidates to full-time officer posts typically use a system of selection by the executive committee [42]. In many white-collar unions this system of appointment is also used for general secretaries [43]. When selection is used, the age of entry into officer posts is younger than the average for unions as a whole [44].

Full-time officers have typically been poorly paid considering the responsibility and scope of their work [45]. Reasons for this include the general feelings that union officers should have a style of life not too far removed from that of their members and that the work has a strong vocational element. However, some white-collar unions, e.g. NALGO and the Civil Service unions, take the opposing view and think that salaries should be sufficiently high to attract suitable potential leaders. This is in line with their policy of external recruitment and leads to the development of professionalism, with union officers being regarded as men with careers.

Full-time officers are, of course, employees of the union and as such need an independent body to negotiate for them on their own terms and conditions of employment. The usual arrangement is to have some form of staff union [46]. In NALGO this arrangement is formalized into a properly constituted Whitley Council.

In addition to full-time officers there are many union members who serve their unions on a voluntary basis in various offices. These include posts such as branch officers, national conference delegates and shop stewards, and in some unions, district officials, national executive committee members, national treasurers and presidents. In these positions they may have a considerable influence on union policies, and in some cases will have contact with local management over claims and grievances. The typical method of appointing lay officers is by election [47].

For white-collar employees who hold part-time union office there is sometimes a problem of role conflict. This is particularly acute for those who are employed as managers since they may be in a situation where, in their work role, they must represent to their subordinates a management with which they, as union officers, are in dispute. However, this apparent role conflict is not necessarily significant. As a part-time union officer, the manager is concerned only with the interests of his own grade and is not necessarily allied with the claims of his subordinates, as a group, against the employer. Furthermore, the conflict of the manager, as an employee, with his employer is inherent, and being a union officer is merely an open manifestation of this conflict and not a cause of it. In fact in addition to his management and his union role, the individual will also have a family role, a political role, and other roles, any of which may promote further conflict for him.

There is the danger, however, that false interpretation of the situation by various parties may lead to a diminished effectiveness of the employee in one of his roles. This would be accentuated if he devoted a disproportionate amount of his time to either his management or his union role. On the other hand, it is conceivable that the manager's own union experience will enable him to understand better the behaviour of his subordinates, and in so doing help him to function as a more effective manager. Indeed this is likely to be the case, since any manager who actively participates in a union is showing a realistic understanding of the industrial system in which he operates. This will lead him to a fuller appreciation of the role of a manager.

In the public sector, many managers hold part-time union office without any apparent detriment to either role. There is no reason to suspect that in the future, with the growth in union membership, the same position will not apply in private industry.

Registration

The Industrial Relations Act 1971 alters the significance of registration. The position existing before this was that under the provisions of the Trade Union Act 1871, unions could register with the Chief Registrar of Friendly Societies. This was not compulsory, but nevertheless at the end of 1970, 326 unions of employees, with a total membership of 9,277,000 were registered [48]. These included most partially white-collar unions (with the exception of UPW) and many white-collar unions, including APECCS, TASS, TSSA, CPSA, NAS.

The reason that some white-collar unions were not registered, e.g. IPCS, NUT, BTOG, probably derived from the fact that registration had traditionally been viewed by many white-collar employees as a sign of militancy in a union. This interpretation had most likely come about because most blue-collar unions were registered, and so registration by a white-collar union was seen as an identification and association with them. A study of attitudes shown by many white-collar unions towards registration illustrates this viewpoint [49].

In fact, registration had no such significance. It merely entitled a union to certain exemptions from income tax in respect of interest and dividends applicable and applied solely for the purpose of provident benefits, and gave it small administrative benefits over, for example, changes in trustees and recovery by the union of its property and effects. In return for these benefits registration placed obligations on unions regarding the scope, but not the content, of their rules: the requirement to notify the registrar of any changes in rules, officers or address; and the requirement to prepare a statement showing assets and liabilities [50].

The reason that most unions registered was not that the advantages so outweighed the obligations, but more as a sign that they were a stable organization wishing to conform to good standards of administration. This more realistic picture of registration had become increasingly recognized by white-collar unions, and explains why more of them were registering.

Some white-collar unions, including NALGO, were certified trade unions under the provisions of the Trade Union Act 1913. Certification placed no obligations on unions [51].

The only practical difference between registered and certified unions on the one hand, and unregistered unions on the other, was that the latter could apparently neither sue nor be sued in contract [52]. The protective provisions of the Trade Union Acts 1871 and 1913, the Conspiracy and Protection of Property Act 1875, and the Trade Disputes Acts 1906 and 1965, applied to all bodies that were legally trade unions, whether they were registered, certified or unregistered.

However, registration now has a new and increased signifi-

cance following the introduction of legislation which, in this
area at least, is based on the broad recommendations of the
Donovan Commission [53]. Under the Industrial Relations Act
1971, a Chief Registrar of Trade Unions and Employers'
Associations has been appointed [54]. Any independent
organization of workers which has the power to alter its own
rules and control the application of its own property and funds
is eligible to apply for registration as a trade union [55].
Organizations which at the time of the passing of the Act were
registered as trade unions under the previous legislation have
been entered on the provisional register for examination by the
registrar of their eligibility for full registration [56].

The Act requires that all organizations of employees, whether
registered or not, follow certain principles of conduct concern-
ing the rights of employees to join the organization and to
participate in it, and lays down the conditions under which
members may be subjected to disciplinary action or have their
membership terminated. Breaches of these principles constitute
an unfair industrial practice [57].

Additionally, registered unions are required to keep certain
financial records, to submit an annual return to the registrar
relating to their affairs, to publish an annual report, and to notify
the registrar of changes in rules, officers, or addresses. The
registrar is empowered to inspect unions to see that they are
performing these duties, and to investigate any complaint
against the conduct of the union [58].

However, registration also confers a number of immunities
and privileges which the Act denies to unregistered organizations. Protection against action for damages for inducing
employees to breach their contract of employment is confined
to registered unions [59]. Although unregistered unions retain
their existing immunity in respect of the tort of conspiracy
when they act in furtherance of an industrial dispute, they are
liable for an action for damages in the new NIRC and there is
no limit set on the amount of compensation [60]. This last point
applies to an action for any unfair industrial practice against an
unregistered union.

The right of an individual to belong to a union of his choice and to take part in its activities applies, in relation to his employer, only to registered unions [61]. Only they can make application to the NIRC that they be recognized as sole bargaining agent [62].

Only registered trade unions may be party to an agency shop agreement or may initiate an application for a ballot to establish such an agreement [63]. The position is similar with an approved closed shop agreement [64]. Application for remedial action where a procedure agreement is inadequate or non-existent, or complaint to the NIRC that an employer has failed to disclose information required by the Act, is limited to registered trade unions [65].

The TUC is strongly opposed to registration and has instructed affiliated unions not to register. This is partly as a plank in its general opposition to the Industrial Relations Act 1971, since for a union to register would be a sign that it is willing to work within the Act, and partly because the TUC regards registration as an unwarranted intrusion into unions' internal affairs. However, some unions organizing white-collar employees see the matter differently. A few have already defied the TUC and have registered, e.g. BALPA, CHSE, NUBE, ESA. Their reasons for so doing are two-fold. First, they acknowledge the instrumental advantages of registration now that the Act is law. In particular white-collar unions could use the Act to win recognition in areas where they are denied it now. Secondly, they fear that by refusing to register they will lose membership and influence to non-TUC affiliated unions and staff associations which have themselves registered.[1]

It is likely that if the Act remains in force in its present form, then unions in general, and those organizing white-collar employees in particular, will register in increasing numbers in order to protect themselves from crippling damages in the event of a strike, and to enable them to use the law to their advantage as much as possible.

---

[1] Non-TUC affiliated unions which have already registered include ALGES, BACM, IPCS. For the position of staff associations, see infra, pp. 105–11.

Affiliation to TUC

Traditionally some unions organizing white-collar employees have opposed affiliation to the TUC either on the grounds that they see political implications in this, or because they see the TUC as a blue-collar union body of little relevance to them [66]. However, these objections are now becoming largely historic and over the years the number of white-collar employees in unions affiliated has increased both absolutely and proportionally. At the end of 1970 white-collar employees composed 7·0 per cent of the total affiliated membership of the TUC, and those in white-collar unions alone made up 20·5 per cent of the total membership.[1]

One factor contributing to this increase is that the political objection to affiliation is seen as less valid. In fact a survey carried out by IPCS in 1963 revealed that none of the major political parties thought that TUC affiliation definitely implied support for the Labour Party [67]. Further to this, some white-collar unions have realized that it is possible to affiliate on a purely industrial basis, and NUBE, for example, stresses that its affiliation is of this type and it abstains from political motions at Annual Congress. Certainly there is no evidence that, as was once thought, affiliation of a union to the TUC leads to a decrease in its white-collar membership because of political objections [68].

However, the main reason for the increasing affiliation to the TUC of unions organizing white-collar employees is the instrumental advantages to be gained. The increasing scale of industrial organizations and the growth of supra-national companies, together with the increasing involvement of the Government in the industrial situation, are making unions realize that in isolation they can exert little influence and cannot therefore effectively further the interests of their members. Thus, for example, NALGO, in the face of the pay pause and

---

[1] See Appendix 4. In fact IPCS and the Society of Civil Servants are the only unions of any size which are not affiliated to the TUC. Affiliated white-collar and partially white-collar unions are listed in Appendices 1 and 2.

the establishment of the National Economic Development Council, sought affiliation as the only possible means of influencing Government policy which bore heavily on the employment of its members [69].

The TUC can exert a strong influence as the sole central body of the trade union movement in Britain, with over 90 per cent of total union membership affiliated to it. As such the TUC is recognized as the spokesman for the movement, and it nominates representatives to numerous international, national, regional and local bodies, including many statutory committees. In all it is represented on over 120 bodies including the National Joint Advisory Council to the Secretary of State for Employment, the National Economic Development Council, and the International Labour Organization [70]. In addition the Government and other bodies seek the views of the TUC on many topics.

White-collar members of affiliated unions can influence the policies of the TUC in two main ways. Appendix 4 shows the present group structure which is the basis for nominations to the General Council, the governing body of the TUC. White-collar union members are more than proportionally represented since white-collar unions, with 20·5 per cent of total TUC membership, have 21·6 per cent of the seats on the General Council (compared with 16·2 per cent of membership and 18·0 per cent of seats at the end of 1968). The second main means of influence is the Non-Manual Workers' Advisory Committee. This has joint membership of representatives from the General Council and from unions catering for white-collar employees, and it reports and makes recommendations on matters of specific concern to white-collar union members [71]. The resolutions of the annual Conference of Unions catering for Non-Manual Workers are implemented either directly by the Committee or through the General Council.

An examination of the debates at the annual Trades Union Congress shows that white-collar employees are playing quite a significant role in shaping policy, although blue-collar unions, with their massive memberships, still dominate the proceedings. However, the growth in union membership among white-collar employees, along with the need for some central body, will, on the assumption that no separate white-collar body is formed, mean that the white-collar employees will come to dominate the TUC in the future.[1]

As the need for the TUC has increased over the years so it has, as a body, been gaining increasing power over affiliated unions. It has expanded its requirements of affiliated unions from adherence to the Bridlington Principles governing spheres of recruitment and poaching of members to include compliance with the General Council's request to return to work in the case of certain unconstitutional stoppages [72]. A further example of its growing control is the circular that it sent to affiliated unions in December 1969 suggesting that they should make detailed provisions within their rules for strike ballots, and calling for a clearer statement of the powers and duties of shop stewards.

These moves were partly an attempt by the TUC to counter demands from successive governments for increasing control over the conduct of unions. Nevertheless legislation has been passed, and the Industrial Relations Act 1971 has several implications for the TUC.

In general it provides an incentive for unity in the trade union movement if a policy of non-co-operation with the Act is to be successful. However in other ways it is having a disruptive influence. The main issue is over registration. Although this offers certain attractions to unions and particularly to those organizing white-collar employees, they face suspension and possible expulsion from the TUC if they fail to comply with its instruction not to register. One of the first examples of this is the threat against NUBE, which has compounded the felony by applying to the NIRC for bargaining rights at United Dominions Trust. It seems unlikely that large-scale expulsions will take place, because such moves would harm the union movement more than they could possibly help it. The situation will, however, act as a disincentive for further white-collar unions to affiliate to the TUC, and lessen the commitment of some affiliated unions to that body. In other ways also, the Act

[1] See also infra, pp. 94–6.

will weaken the position of the TUC. For example, the legislation establishes procedures for dealing with inter-union disputes which conflict with the rules set out in the Bridlington Agreement.

Political Activities

Political action has for many years been viewed by some unions as a valuable additional method to industrial action for furthering the interests of their members. Through it unions seek to ensure that both public opinion and the law are sympathetic to growth in trade union membership and influence. It offers them the promise of a means of overcoming the economic imbalance between employer and employees which limits the effectiveness of industrial action, and has the advantage that it can exert an influence in areas where unions have weak bargaining power.

To engage in political activities a union must, under the Trade Union Act 1913, obtain a majority in favour in a ballot vote before establishing a political fund, and all political objectives have to be met out of this separate fund. At the end of 1970, 102 unions of employees had political objects, with 6,738,000 members contributing to political funds [73]. These included most partially white-collar unions but only a few white-collar unions, e.g. ASTMS, TASS, APECCS. Under the Trade Disputes and Trade Union Act 1946, union members have the right to contract-out of paying the political levy, and at the end of 1969, 20·3 per cent of members were contracted-out [74].

A few unions use their political funds for general lobbying and for helping candidates of any political party who will pay special attention to the union's sphere of interest.[1] The majority of unions do, however, support the Labour Party. The main method of support is through affiliation, which involves financial support through affiliation fees and practical support by sending delegates to the Labour Party Conference and by nominating representatives for the 12 trade union seats on the 26-seat National Executive Committee of the Labour Party. In the

[1] This was the case in AScW before its merger with ASSET.

early 1960s all but 5 unions with political funds were affiliated, but by 1969 only 68 unions were affiliated to the Labour Party out of the 108 with political funds. This decrease is due partly to the special circumstances of this period, including the Labour Government's incomes policy and the proposed 'penal clauses' in the White Paper *In Place of Strife*, but may also indicate a new trend. However, many unions that affiliate to the Labour Party do so only on a part of their political membership. In 1955, for example, NUPE affiliated only 64 per cent and CHSE only 26 per cent [75]. In 1968 the Labour Party received less than one-third of the total union political funds through affiliation fees.

The other main ways in which unions support the Labour Party are by contributions to its 'Fighting Fund' at the time of general elections, and by sponsoring certain selected Labour Party Parliamentary candidates. TSSA is one of the few white-collar unions which sponsors candidates, but many partially white-collar unions do, including TGWU which in 1969 supported 27 MPs. The money given is for help with election expenses and day-to-day running of the constituency. In return, sponsored MPs are expected to keep a watch on subjects of interest to the union and to fight for the union's policy.

Unions that are affiliated to the TUC have a further link with the Labour Party through the National Council of Labour. However, this is a purely deliberative body and does not make policy [76].

It is the traditional link between political objectives and support for the Labour Party that deters many white-collar unions from establishing political funds, e.g. NALGO, CPSA. They argue either that the majority of their members are not supporters of the Labour Party, or that the minority of members who are not supporters would leave the union if it engaged in political activities. (Contrast this with Japan, where the political sympathies of white-collar unions lie strongly with socialist parties [77].) However, it is possible for a union to have a political fund and remain independent of any party, and there is no evidence that establishing a political fund does lead to a fall in membership [78]. A few other unions organizing white-collar

employees do not have a political fund as they see no necessary
connection between unionism and politics, e.g. NUBE. A
survey among qualified members of AScW revealed that 50 per
cent of respondents shared this attitude [79].

Other unions for white-collar employees see instrumental
advantages in engaging in political activities and supporting the
Labour Party. They argue that if it is in their interests to align
with the industrial wing of the workers' movement, i.e. the
TUC, then in the political and social field they should align
with the political wing of the same movement. In those unions
that are affiliated to the Labour Party there exists the right of
members to contract-out of the political levy; in APECCS
some 16 per cent [80] have contracted-out and in TSSA a
smaller percentage, while 63 per cent [81] of TASS members
and 44 per cent [82] of ASTMS members have contracted-out.
Explanations for these figures include political apathy in
APECCS, a pro-Labour tradition in TSSA, and perhaps a
strong left-wing element in TASS who are critical of the last
Labour Government's policies.

The effectiveness of political action for those unions that
have no links with the Labour Party is likely to be limited. This
is because such unions are confined to general lobbying and the
support of individual MPs whose primary responsibilities lie
with their parties and their constituents.

This is why most unions with political funds align themselves
with the Labour Party, but even here there are limits to the
extent that they can influence policy. The Parliamentary
Labour Party is largely autonomous, and neither the National
Executive Committee nor the Conference are able to dictate to
Labour MPs or Labour Governments. Similarly unions cannot
ask their sponsored MPs to make any formal promises that they
will help them, since their responsibilities lie with the Parliamentary Labour Party and their constituents. There is some
evidence from previous Labour Governments that union
influence is determined primarily by their economic strength
as with other Governments [83].

Nevertheless, the unions control the bulk of the Labour
Party's income, and on those rare occasions when they present

a united front on a political issue they form a very influential pressure group. Thus in 1969 the unions were able to make the Labour Government reverse its policy over the 'penal clauses' in its proposed industrial relations legislation [84].

In the future, as Government influence over the conduct of industry increases in areas such as industrial relations, training, the location of industry, monopolies, so will unions increasingly need to exert an influence over these political decisions. The relative balance between industrial and political action as a means of exerting this influence, and the nature of political action, is not entirely clear. On some issues the unions have relied largely on legislation, for example, over the implementation of equal pay for women, while on other issues they prefer to concentrate on industrial action, for example over the issue of a national minimum wage. Most unions preferred to use political action to oppose the passage of the Conservative Government's Industrial Relations Bill.

On the question of the form of political activity, experience with the last Labour Government over Prices and Incomes Policy and the proposed 'penal clauses' indicates a growing political independence on the part of the unions. For its part, the Labour Party, and more particularly a Labour Government, must consider the interests of the country as a whole and not just those of the union movement, and therefore its views can never coincide exclusively with those of the unions.

However, the alternatives to some form of association with the Labour Party are not very attractive to the union movement. An attachment to the Conservative Party, even if some mechanism for collective affiliation existed, would fail in that the interests of many of that Party's supporters run exactly counter to those of trade unions. The remaining strategy of seeking political advantage on an *ad hoc* basis is impracticable since there is no guarantee to a political party that a union can deliver the votes and so keep its part of any bargain which is struck. Therefore the trade union movement is likely to retain some form of association with the Labour Party, and the latter will remain reluctant to offend the unions outright since it needs their finance and their votes, and will therefore continue to be willing to offer them, to some extent at least, a political platform. Of course, at the same time, the unions will be careful to retain contacts, particularly through the TUC, which give them channels of communication with all Governments, Conservative as well as Labour.[1]

As the need for some form of political activity is increasing, so are the possible objections of white-collar union members to establishing a political fund decreasing. Unions are becoming more politically independent, while the remaining link with the Labour Party is becoming more tolerable as the Party itself becomes more attractive to some white-collar employees. For example, out of the 363 Labour MPs elected in the 1966 General Election, more than 200 belonged to the middle-class professions. It therefore seems likely that political activities among unions catering for white-collar employees will become more widespread.

Affiliation to White-Collar Bodies

The principal white-collar body in Britain is the NFPW, which has affiliated to it some 27 white-collar unions and the white-collar sections of 13 partially white-collar unions, giving it a total membership of over one million [85]. It is, above all, a forum for the discussion of problems of common interest to unions for white-collar employees, and decisions taken by its annual conference are implemented by its executive committee.

The most important characteristic of the NFPW is that it has good relationships with the TUC and seeks to avoid any conflict or duplication with that body. Most of the unions affiliated to the NFPW are also affiliated to the TUC, while the former body has a representative on the TUC Non-Manual Workers' Advisory Committee. In fact the NFPW's limited finance and lack of a research department mean that action is often taken through the TUC.

Those unions which affiliate to the NFPW do so to gain information, advice and support from other unions organizing white-collar employees. However, some unions have doubts as to the usefulness of NFPW with its limited finance and in-

[1] Supra, pp. 87–8.

fluence or, like IPCS, deplore its lack of independence from the TUC, and so do not affiliate.

It is the generally weak position of the NFPW that has led, from time to time, to attempts to form a representative white-collar body, independent of the TUC. In 1962 the Conference of Professional and Public Service Organizations (COPPSO) was established to represent 600,000 white-collar union members. This body had very limited objectives and failed after only about one year partly because the Government refused to give it representation on bodies such as NEDC and because NALGO, its founding member, decided to affiliate to the TUC [86].

It seems likely that in the future there will remain just one central body in the British trade union movement, namely the TUC. This situation differs from other countries, e.g. Germany, Sweden, which have separate white-collar central bodies [87]. Arguments in favour of a separate white-collar central body stress that some problems are virtually unique to unions catering for white-collar employees, for example the general relationship between productivity and comparability, while on other issues there is a divergence of interest between white-collar and blue-collar employees, for example over payment differentials.[1] They also see the TUC as dominated by blue-collar unions.

However, the arguments for retaining just one central body are stronger. All unions share some common interests, e.g. high employment, and as a unified movement they will be best able to deal with a changing situation in the interests of all union members. For example, on the factor of technical change a separate blue-collar union central body would have to exert a policy of negative resistance which would be harmful in the long term both to its members and to white-collar employees. In this situation a unified movement is better able to take a more constructive attitude to further the interests of its members and is in a stronger position to deal with employers and the Government than a divided and weakened movement. Similarly a single central body is better able to cope with the shift in the

[1] Supra, pp. 47–51.

labour force from blue-collar to white-collar employees; and its internal composition should reflect this swing.

Although there is some divergence of interests between white-collar employees and blue-collar employees, these are really no greater than the differences existing within the groups. Sectional interests are more effectively dealt with by pressure groups within the TUC than by breakaway bodies, since the former has established channels of communication and contacts with interested parties.

Some white-collar unions are members of international white-collar bodies. For example, BAC is a member of the chemical industry's international federation of executives (FICCIA), which investigates and reports on general terms and conditions of employment. With the growth of international companies such contacts will become more valuable, but only within the general framework of the relations between the TUC and the International Confederation of Free Trade Unions.

Relations with Employers

Unions for white-collar employees seek to protect and further the interests of their members in their relationships with employers, as do all unions. In so doing unions are concerned with terms and conditions of employment and an increasing range of managerial relations [88]. They are beginning to seek a voice in the making of decisions which will affect the future status and security of their members. These include the forward planning of manpower requirements, industrial training, and job and income security [89].

The main ways in which relations with employers take place are through joint consultation and collective bargaining. The former is largely confined to the local level and has had a chequered history [90]. It is largely regarded by unions as being of little importance and is unlikely to survive as a separate institution. Rather it will be consolidated into a single channel of representation in which the majority of topics are the subject of collective bargaining, but in which a few, such as safety, remain genuinely topics for joint consultation. Collective bargaining is, and will probably continue to be, the main means for the conduct of relations between unions organizing white-collar employees and employers. Theoretically there are two separate aspects of collective bargaining: the negotiation of improved terms and conditions of employment, and the settlement of issues arising over the interpretation of existing procedural and substantive agreements. However, the distinction between these two processes is not always clear and there is overlap in the procedural machinery.

In the public sector negotiations for improved terms and conditions generally take place at national level. For teachers there are the Burnham Committees which are composed of teachers' representatives (i.e. the unions), management representatives (i.e. the local authorities) and Government representatives (i.e. the Department of Education and Science), together with an independent chairman. Effectively the management side retains the majority vote on matters affecting the overall cost of a new salary award, but not on its distribution. There is a provision for compulsory arbitration, but Parliament can, when certain 'weighty' reasons exist, sway this award. Recently, concern about the operation of the Burnham machinery has been expressed by all parties to it. The key point at issue is the role of the Secretary of State for Education and Science [91].

For the Civil Service the overall negotiating body is the National Whitley Council, which has a 'Staff side' made up of union representatives and an 'Official side' made up of heads of departments and representatives from the Treasury. In the case of failure to reach agreement recourse can be made to the Civil Service Arbitration Tribunal which has an independent chairman and panels of members from both sides. Below the National Whitley Council are Departmental Councils [92]. One effect of this machinery is to place some Treasury officials on the 'Official side' of the Council in cases involving pay increases for their own grades [93].

In local government, most white-collar employees come under the National Joint Council for Local Authorities' Administrative, Professional, Technical and Clerical Services. Here the employers' side is made up of elected representatives of local government such as councillors. The position is similar in the

D

National Health Service with its one general and nine functional Whitley Councils [94].

Within these general frameworks there are grievance procedures which are characterized by the movement of unresolved questions of interpretation of agreements from local to national joint bodies.

In the private sector there are few industry-wide procedural agreements relating to white-collar employees. One exception was in engineering and here the white-collar unions, although affiliated to the Confederation of Shipbuilding and Engineering Unions, negotiated separately from the blue-collar unions. However, the engineering national agreement was terminated at the end of 1971. In those industries where there is no national machinery, bargaining for improved terms and conditions takes place at plant or company level; and grievance procedures, although typically not closely defined, channel unresolved issues up to this level [95].

In collective bargaining disputes inevitably sometimes occur. The way in which a dispute is manifested depends partly on the procedural machinery within the organization and whether or not this contains provisions for arbitration, partly on the role of the Government through the conciliation and arbitration services of the DE, and partly on the attitudes and circumstances of the union involved.

The type and extent of industrial action taken by unions for white-collar employees varies quite considerably. NALGO, although it has a provision that if 90 per cent of a branch concerned in a dispute are in favour then a strike can take place, has never carried out any industrial action more severe than an overtime ban. One reason for this is that members do not want to tarnish their image as public servants, and this feeling is accentuated by NALGO having amongst its members some senior grades of employees who exert a disproportionate influence on its policies [96]. Other reasons for this lack of militancy are instrumental and include the facts that having a vertical structure NALGO cannot so easily find support within the union to promote a strong sectional claim, that the length of notice required by some officials would destroy all elements of surprise and make a strike less effective, and that a strike might endanger superannuation rights.

CPSA has never called a strike, although it has provisions for doing so. This is partly due to the fact that pay is mainly set on the basis of fair comparisons as established by a survey carried out by the Civil Service Pay Research Unit, and in the event of disagreement over this or any other matter there is recourse to an Arbitration Tribunal. However, it was the threat of a 'work-to-rule' in 1961–2 that led to the Government allowing the independence of the Tribunal. Similarly, TSSA has committed itself to arbitration, but has retained the strike weapon as a last resort.

NUBE, although it changed its rules in 1960 to require only a simple majority of those concerned in order that strike action can be taken, shows relatively little militancy. This is largely due to the fact that in the clearing banks it has an average membership density of below 40 per cent, making the successful conduct of large-scale strikes very difficult [97]. In the Trustee Savings Banks, where the density of membership is higher, NUBE took strike action in 1962–3.

TASS has called many strikes and sees them as a '. . . valuable means of furthering members' interests . . . where negotiations fail to produce an acceptable settlement' [98]. It is able to act in this way because its members are employed in positions where withdrawal of their labour is highly disruptive. Furthermore the broadly horizontal structure of the union means that it can exert pressure on any one plant or firm without financially crippling itself. Thus in Rolls–Royce in 1969–70 the tactics used by TASS were to submit a claim at one plant and to win this if necessary by calling out key design staff, and then to repeat the process in other plants of the company on the grounds of parity.

ASTMS shares a similar position with TASS on industrial action and also prefers to concentrate its activities on leading corporations which it sees as pacemakers for the rest of industry. BALPA has called several strikes since these can 'ground' an airline and give the union a very strong bargaining position. APECCS engages in strike action where it has a high membership density. Most partially white-collar unions are prepared to engage in strike action to further their claims.

The record of industrial action by teachers' unions can be largely explained by the ambiguous status position of the occupation. An examination of the constituent elements of which professional status can be regarded as being composed shows that at the present teachers are in a weak position on many counts, for example, their length of education and training [99]. Thus the problem for teachers' organizations has been to decide whether to concentrate on trade union activities to improve their economic position and general standing, or whether such action is incompatible with professional status.[1]

The NAS has often used strike action, regarding it as a means of gaining publicity for its cause and of influencing opinion. On the other hand NUT, for many years, tried to satisfy both the need for a professional body to promote educational progress and the need for a trade union, and in trying to carry out a dual role may not have been very successful in either [100].[2] Apart from some local strikes in the period around World War I, until recently NUT spurned strike action as inconsistent with its claim to be a professional body, although it did threaten mass resignations in a dispute with Durham County Council in 1950–2. The tactics it had actually used were no more extreme than withdrawal from collecting National Savings in schools [101].

However, a combination of factors led to NUT engaging in a programme of strike action during 1969–70 which resulted in the award of a considerable interim pay settlement. The particular circumstances of the claim centred about the collapse of the Government's incomes policy, but underlying this was a

---

[1] In the United States, a local of the American Federation of Teachers involved in an abortive strike tried to maintain an aura of professionalism in the eyes of the community, but in its internal relations used the same tactics as blue-collar unions. See D. S. Hamermesh, 'Professional and White-Collar Unionism', *Industrial Relations*, October 1966, pp. 118–19.

[2] Professional activities are discussed infra, pp. 103–5. It is interesting to compare teachers with the medical profession, who first fought for professional status through the establishment of the General Medical Council and are now able to concentrate on achieving a high standard of living through the BMA. See infra, pp. 115–18.

general dissatisfaction. There is also little doubt that in taking this action the teachers were influenced by increasing militancy among white-collar employees in general, and by developments in the public sector [102]. The campaign was only successful, however, because of the unity achieved on this occasion by the NUT, NAS and AMA. A feature of the campaign was the attempt by the NUT to gain maximum publicity [103]. One example was a full-page advertisement in the press headed, 'Full-time teacher wanted. Starting salary £13 a week' [104].

Most unions organizing white-collar employees are unwilling to be used for blacklegging or strike-breaking activities by employers in the event of a blue-collar union dispute. NALGO and ASTMS, for example, have specific policies on this [105].

The new legislation on industrial relations could bring about some fundamental changes in the relations between unions and employers. The proposals are variously viewed as likely to promote good industrial relations, as being totally irrelevant, or as being likely to lead to disruption of relations between employers and employees. Their actual impact will be determined by the extent to which the provisions are invoked by employers, unions and the Government.

The Act provides for the Secretary of State, an employer, or specific registered trade unions to be able to make an application to the NIRC that a procedure agreement is defective or does not exist, and following a report of the CIR any party covered by the recommendations may apply for them to be made legally binding [106]. However, the provision is likely to have little impact since any procedure agreement which is not voluntarily accepted by all parties to it is unlikely to improve the conduct of collective bargaining, while the TUC is anxious to avoid the possibility of a union having a legally enforceable procedure imposed upon it.

A further provision in the Act is that written collective agreements will be legally enforceable contracts unless they contain a provision to the contrary, and that it will be unfair industrial practice to break such an agreement [107]. Although designed to reduce the number of strikes taking place, legally enforceable agreements could result in unions becoming increasingly militant in their relations with employers since by taking a moderate settlement unions would lay themselves open to be sued for damages if their members broke this agreement. However, it is unlikely that many legally binding agreements will be signed. The TUC has advised that if necessary a union could take industrial action for the purpose of securing an exclusion clause, providing it was acting in contemplation or furtherance of an industrial dispute, while many employers also show little inclination to enter into such agreements.

Before the passing of the Industrial Relations Act 1971 some white-collar unions operated forms of a closed shop agreement (e.g. NUJ, Equity) while others favoured its introduction on moral and instrumental grounds (e.g. TASS, BALPA, TSSA) [108]. However, under the Act any existing pre-entry closed shop agreements become void, and any attempts to induce employers to introduce them is an unfair industrial practice, although provisions are made for the establishment of agency shop agreements and approved closed shop agreements [109].

These provisions would cause little change to registered unions, and indeed the arrangement for approved closed shop agreements was specifically inserted to help unions such as Equity, which organize in occupations where employment is typically casual and of short duration, and where employees are open to exploitation [110]. Those unions which decide not to register will have to rely on their capacity to recruit members on a voluntary basis, and so will be at a disadvantage in comparison with registered unions. An example is the case of BALPA which has registered and applied to the NIRC for an agency shop agreement. If this is granted it will prevent the growth of the Professional Pilots' Association which broke away from BALPA and is now seeking links with ASTMS.

By providing a system for unions to gain recognition, the Act aims to eliminate recognition strikes. The effect of this will be reduced by those unions which do not register, since they will have to rely on the traditional methods of putting pressure on the employer to gain recognition. Perhaps the existence of the legislation may, in the long term, lead to a more willing acceptance of unions for white-collar employees in the private sector.

The provisions for disclosure of information to union representatives by employers could aid the development of collective bargaining in the field of managerial relations but, here again, the provision applies only to registered unions [111].

Underlying this whole discussion is the question of the ability of an unregistered union to take strike action without committing an unfair industrial practice. It would seem that to do this it must avoid inducing a breach of contract, which can only be done by an employee giving due notice and by ensuring that the strike is not in breach of any term of his contract of employment [112]. Only time will show whether this is possible.

Thus, in its early stages of operation at least, the provisions of the Act are unlikely to be fully used. If operated vigorously the effect of the Act would be to introduce an inflexibility into the relations between unions organizing white-collar employees and employers, and in the event of recourse being made to the NIRC in any situation, some bitterness would be introduced. The proposals go no way to tackling the basic causes of disputes.

In the longer-term future, a further way in which relations with employers might take place is by having trade unions nominate representatives to serve on the boards of companies. This scheme has the support of the TUC and of many individual unions, and was favoured by the last Labour Government [113]. If it is to be introduced and if it is to be effective, problems of the responsibility of the workers' director and his possible remoteness from the majority of employees will have to be overcome [114]. This move could herald a radical change in the legal position of companies, making them responsible to their employees as well as to their shareholders.

Professional Activities and Services

In addition to their principal protective function, many unions organizing white-collar employees seek to assist their members in further ways.

One of these may be dubbed as professional activities, and involves an overall attempt to improve the professional status of the occupation. Thus ATTI seeks '... to advance further and higher education ... [and] ... to maintain standards of professional conduct' [115]. In order to accomplish this it wants teacher representation on all bodies bearing on further education, and demands a larger share of the national income for education and fullest educational opportunities for all young people. NUBE includes among its objects the wish '... to maintain the highest possible standard of service given by its members to the public and the Banking Industry and by such Industry to the public and the community' [116].

NUT, along with other teachers' unions, has for many years been active in campaigning for a lengthening of the period of training required to qualify as a teacher, and for final withdrawal of permission to employ any unqualified persons on teaching duties [117]. To some extent the James Report, which recommends that teaching become an all graduate profession, marks a success in this field [118]. Another area where teachers' unions have pushed for professional status is by the establishment of a Teachers' General Council, the main functions of which would be to determine standards of entry, to keep a register of teachers, and to assume responsibility for professional discipline. Although a Council has been established in Scotland, the exact form proposed for England and Wales was not acceptable to the NUT [119]. However, unlike other professions, teachers' unions have constantly demanded an increase in the number of teachers [120].[1]

By engaging in such professional activities unions are more likely to be viewed as more responsible bodies by white-collar employees, by employers, and by the Government. Their function is seen as broadened from a position of solely self-centred advancement to one of concern with their industry as a whole. This enhanced status of the union makes its recruitment of members an easier task and advances members' individual status along with that of the occupation. It may also help the union to be more effective in carrying out its protective function.

---

[1] Compare this position with other professions, infra, pp. 112–13.

Another way in which unions help their members is by providing a range of services for the use of individual members. NALGO has probably the most comprehensive range, and offers legal advice, special reduced price purchasing facilities for a wide range of goods and services, a holiday service, a vocational education service, a benevolent fund, the NALGO Provident Society, an insurance company for members (LOGOMIA), and a special connection with a building society. TASS produces and sells approximately 100,000 technical booklets and data sheets each year, and also offers an employment service through *TASS News* [121]. Other unions offer similar services.

The aim of these services is to cater for the union member as a consumer as well as an employee, and so to retain existing members and attract new ones. However, it seems likely that any effect of these services will be very minor compared with a union's effectiveness in its protective function. Indeed the necessity for certain welfare and educational services in our welfare society is worth questioning, and a cost–benefit analysis of some of these services might well point to the discontinuance of them. The union's limited resources would probably be better concentrated around serving the employment interests of its members. However, some observers point out that TASS's technical publications have won it support from sections of the white-collar labour force which would normally be alienated by its militancy.

STAFF ASSOCIATIONS

General Characteristics

Staff associations are each confined to the employees of one company, and as such they may be considered as closed bodies. They have basically vertical structures, containing various different grades in their membership, and they are generally confined to white-collar employees. Their internal organizations usually follow the physical and administrative divisions of the companies within which they exist, and provisions for the representation of identifiable groups, e.g. departments, are

D*

generally made. This often takes the form of nominating a representative to an executive committee.

All staff associations were established on the initiative of an employer, mostly with the aim of combating the spread of trade unions [122]. All the officers come from within the employing organization and most of them are part-time, but in some staff associations a full-time officer is found. However, staff associations are seldom financially independent since all officers are effectively paid by the company. This factor, coupled with the fact that the employer has the right to choose who he will employ and has direct dismissal rights over all staff association members except the very few full-time officers, explains how the employer can dominate the staff association.

It is not surprising, therefore, that staff associations subscribe to a unitary frame of reference [123]. They see their interests as being common with those of their employer, and they trust in his readiness to acknowledge and rectify any rightful grievances that they may raise. Staff associations therefore reject the need for any kinds of sanctions, seeing them as irrelevant. In fact, of course, their dependence on the employer and their internalism means that there are no sanctions that they, as corporate bodies, can bring to bear.

Thus in most companies staff associations have consultative and advisory powers only. They are prepared to give their opinion on topics such as changes in working methods, fringe benefits and employee facilities, but do not generally enter into the nebulous area of 'managerial prerogative'. Most of them regard salaries as an individual matter between employer and employee. In those few companies which do allow their staff associations to negotiate, only one allows disputes to be submitted to independent arbitration, and in all other cases the company is the final court of appeal [124]. Nevertheless, in order to keep their employees from joining trade unions, employers have to offer fairly good terms and conditions of employment and have to make the staff associations appear as effective within their sphere of activity.

Staff associations are internal bodies having relations with one employer only. As such they apparently have no need of, and do not have, relationships with any other staff associations,[1] with trade unions, with political parties, or with the Government through any of its many agencies. Also, because they are confined to one employer and offer no continuity of membership when an employee changes his employment, staff associations offer few, if any, of the welfare benefits associated with trade unions. In this case such benefits are more appropriately provided by the employer.

The Industrial Relations Act 1971 is bringing about changes in the position of staff associations. The Act gives any employee the right to become a member of a registered trade union, and includes a procedure to enable such unions to gain recognition.[2] In those areas where unions do register, this provision could lead to the decline of staff associations as distinct bodies. Although the general acceptance by staff associations of the existing power structure in the employing organization makes them attractive to some white-collar employees,[3] this factor is of minor and diminishing importance compared with their perceived effectiveness. Trade unions will exploit the fundamental weakness of staff associations, namely their dependence on concessions from the employer, and will claim that they can better serve the employees' interests. In this situation employers, realizing that they cannot effectively discriminate against union membership, may be unwilling to make large enough concessions to staff associations to enable these to combat the challenge.

The only course of action then open to staff associations if they wish to survive as corporate bodies will be to become independent of employers, to register and to function as internal trade unions. However, their lack of outside connections means that they could have no influence over the many external factors affecting the employment situation of their members, e.g. Government legislation, while their internal nature would make any industrial action financially crippling. To overcome these weaknesses, staff associations would have to group

[1] The bank staff associations are an exception. See infra, p. 110.
[2] Supra, pp. 63–4 and 85–6.
[3] Supra, pp. 30–4.

together and develop external connections. Rather than do this their membership is more likely to become absorbed into existing unions. The decision of the Male and Female Prudential Staff Associations, just before the passing of the Act, to join ASTMS is an indication of what could happen.

The decision of many unions not to register is providing the opportunity for staff associations in those sectors to register as trade unions and use the provisions of the Act to their own advantage. To do so they must assume at least nominal independence. An example is British Insulated Callenders Cables Staff Association which is seeking to register and may then apply to the NIRC to be recognized as a sole bargaining agent. This would thwart the attempt of ASTMS to organize in this area.

Bank Staff Associations

The staff associations in banking are worthy of special study since they are the largest and most publicized ones. They are not, however, typical in every aspect.

Bank staff associations were founded by the various banks in the early 1920s to hinder the growth of NUBE, and initially they depended on the banks for financial support. Their objects are typically stated as '... to enable representatives of the association to exercise their rights of direct access to the Chairman and General Managers and through them to the Board of Directors; to foster a spirit of mutual confidence and goodwill between the Staff, the Management and the Directorate; and to further the interests of the bank and staff' [125]. The constitutions of bank staff associations contain no provisions for any form of industrial action or engagement in political activities.

However, over the years bank staff associations have become increasingly independent. In response to the Conditions of Employment and National Arbitration Order 1940 – Order 1305 – they became subscription-paying bodies with the banks' support in order to prevent NUBE forcing recognition. This change acted to give bank staff associations a sense of identity and marked the first step away from employer domination.

Thus in the period 1953–6 they were able to win the concession from most of the major clearing banks of an agreement allowing independent arbitration in the event of deadlock [126].

Even so, the special characteristics of staff associations makes their independence, even in banking, open to question. Their membership is confined to the employees of one employer, and although this is justified as appropriate to the special circumstances of banking, including non-transferability of staff between banks, it does make it easy for an employer to exert influence if he wishes. This applies particularly to the officials of the association whose salaries are paid, at least in part, by the bank, and who will receive their pensions from this source [127]. There are objections to 'paid organizers from outside' on the grounds of lack of necessary specialist knowledge and because matters of security are at stake. The internal organization of bank staff associations enhances the possibility of employers being able to exert pressure on them. They have no local branches or delegate conference, and instead individual members elect local committees, which in turn elect district committees which in turn elect a central committee. This is the governing body of the association and it appoints the general secretary and other officials. The result of this organizational structure is that individual members are further divorced from the leadership than in most trade unions and that the officials therefore have more power.

In 1962 NUBE complained to the ILO that bank staff associations were under employer control and were used as a device to prevent the union from exercising its function. The subsequent Cameron Inquiry found that this complaint was not justified and that it was the fact that the staff associations prevented NUBE achieving national and exclusive representation which was the real cause of hostility [128]. Both the Cameron Report and the later NBPI Report concluded that the staff associations had done reasonably well for their members on the criteria of achievement, e.g. salaries, fringe benefits, and the former stressed the intense activity of the staff associations in the face of opposition from the employers [129].

However, it is not possible to know how many actions of the

staff associations and concessions by the employers are due to the influence of NUBE. Certainly staff associations were historically supported by the employers as the lesser of two evils and it is a fact that where they have been most vigorous in their activities the membership density of NUBE is lowest [130].

The open indication in the early 1960s by several banks that a salary rise was a point of national agreement among them gave a stimulus to the development of further independence by the bank staff associations. The immediate effect was to lead to the invoking of the independent arbitration machinery for the first time in an attempt to overcome the restriction of internalism and exert an influence throughout the industry [131]. However, in the longer term, as it became obvious that they were being left without any real influence over the terms and conditions of employment of their members, the situation led to the bank staff associations' eventual participation in the joint national negotiating machinery established following the Cameron Inquiry [132]. To do this they transformed the old Central Council of Bank Staff Associations, which was a medium for discussion of points of common interest, into the Council of Bank Staff Associations, which became their representative on the joint council. The CBSA registered as a trade union under the Trade Union Act 1871.

Thus the bank staff associations, through the CBSA, have evolved to the stage where they have overcome the limits of strict internalism and now have aims very similar to those of unions. This development, which has been a result of strict necessity, has been possible because of the unique structure of the banking industry which is made up of a small number of employers each of which has sponsored their own staff association, and in which conditions are very homogeneous.

Faced by this development of the bank staff associations, it is not surprising that NUBE has registered under the Industrial Relations Act 1971. The future of the bank staff associations depends solely on how effective they are perceived to be by their members. At the moment they have no provisions for sanctions against employers and no affiliations with outside bodies, and are therefore in a weaker bargaining position than NUBE.

Furthermore their internal organizations do not lend themselves to high membership participation. However, the possible expulsion of NUBE from the TUC evens the balance between the two organizations to some extent.

It seems likely that in the future the staff associations and NUBE will increasingly come to act in similar ways, and at some stage a merger may well take place between them to form one large union for the banking industry. Failure of the staff associations to be as effective as NUBE will lead to a fall in their membership and the same long-term result as before, namely a single union for all organized employees in banking.

PROFESSIONAL ASSOCIATIONS

General Characteristics

Those professional associations which fall under the definition of white-collar unionism are independent bodies which aim to advance the standing of their professions and allied to this the status and economic interests of their members.[1] Each professional association is confined to one profession and therefore has a broadly horizontal structure with members in salaried employment in various organizations and in independent fee paid practice.

The methods used by professional associations to further the interests of their members are determined largely by their legal position, their ideology, and whether their members are typically employees or not.

Legally, most professional associations are either incorporated under the Companies Acts, e.g. BMA, or have been granted a Royal Charter, e.g. RIBA [133]. This status is inconsistent with trade union status, and such professional associations were not registered under the Trade Union Act 1871. However, they circumnavigated these legal constraints in two main ways. One was to carry out salary surveys and to publish these and discuss them with employers, as an indirect way of influencing salaries [134].[2] The other main way was to set up separate bodies

[1] See supra, p. 21.
[2] Infra, pp. 118–21.

specifically to carry out trade union activities, e.g. RIBA transformed its Salaried and Official Architects Committee into the independent Association of Official Architects [135].

There are a few exceptions to this general pattern. Two professional associations, the Institution of Water Engineers and the Institute of Hospital Engineers, were included in the DE's *Index of Trade Unions*. Both have their membership almost exclusively in the public sector, and as the most representative bodies for certain grades they were prevailed upon to negotiate for them. Other professional associations have sponsored new separate trade unions to carry out their protective function, as in the example of BACM which was founded on the initiative of the Institute of Mining Surveyors and other professional bodies.

The Industrial Relations Act 1971 allows professional associations which are either limited companies or organizations incorporated by charter or letters patent to continue to carry out trade union type activities by establishing a special register. The provisions of the Act apply to organizations on the special register in the same way as they do to registered trade unions with the exception of certain minor administrative points [136]. BMA, BDA and RCN are among professional bodies to have applied for inclusion in the special register. BACM has registered as a trade union under the Act.

The indirect methods that the majority of professional associations were obliged to adopt until very recently because of their legal position are, in fact, in sympathy with their ideology. They are anxious to enhance the esteem in which their profession is publicly held and do not wish to appear overtly to be selfishly pursuing their own interests. Thus methods of unilateral regulation, such as control over entrance to a profession and over the duties of a professional which are adopted by professional associations, can be justified as ensuring the public high levels of competence and high standards of conduct by professionals. Of course these same controls act to increase the status of the profession by giving it an air of exclusiveness and at the same time increase the level of payment which professionals are able to command. Coupled with the setting out of minimum fees for services rendered by independent practitioners, these controls serve to eliminate competition within the profession and safeguard the prospects of members of the profession. Examples of unilateral regulation include the exclusive right of barristers to appear as advocates in higher courts to the exclusion of solicitors, and the refusal of doctors to accept auxiliaries qualified to carry out simpler medical tasks.

As professionals are in increasing numbers becoming salaried employees in both the public and private sectors, professional associations are establishing relationships with employers in order to exert influence over terms and conditions of employment. Architecture is an example of a profession where more than half the members are now employed by public bodies, while in engineering salaried employment has been predominant for many years.

Broadly speaking, most professional associations accept the claims to legitimacy of the ruling group, i.e. the employers.[1] They are therefore concerned primarily with market relations and are involved with managerial relations only to the extent that they will resist any attempt to require their members to act unprofessionally. They also typically show low militancy since they rely on the reasonableness of employers to correct any shortcomings when these are pointed out. On those occasions when professional associations do use sanctions against employers, they are careful to act in ways which will cause the minimum damage to their status. They have never used strike action [137].

In carrying out their activities, professional associations typically remain isolated from each other and from trade unions and staff associations even though these might all have membership in any one employing organization. The main reason for this is that professional organizations view themselves as independent bodies with few common interests with any other organizations. They visualize their own profession as operating largely within a vacuum, unaffected by other professions or by market trends.

[1] Supra, pp. 32–3.

Professional associations do have some exchange of ideas with the Government, but except where it also has the role of employer these do not take place through any formal channels. Generally consultations are confined to matters of specific concern to the particular profession, and on general matters of government policy which might have an indirect effect on professionals, as on other groups of employees, no communication between the professional association and the Government generally takes place. Professional associations do not view these latter matters as within their range of interest.

It is consistent with this ideology that professional associations have no formal connections with any political party. Some of them do, however, have 'interested members' to represent their views in Parliament, e.g. BMA.

Since professional associations cater for their members throughout their working lives, it is not surprising that they, like trade unions, provide a wide range of services. These typically include a technical information service, the publication of a journal, an individual advisory service on matters directly or indirectly concerned with employment, discount trading facilities, and a range of social activities.

The proportion of professionals who are salaried employees is likely to increase as a result of the growth of larger public and private corporations, and of the expansion of specialist professional firms precluding partnerships for many. Thus the status of a profession will depend predominantly on the salary its members can command and the independence they are allowed in carrying out their functions. The success of professional associations will be measured by the extent to which they achieve this. Failure will result in their members joining trade unions.

It therefore seems likely that in the future professional associations will bargain harder with employers and will use such sanctions as are available and necessary to further their claims. Professional associations are already showing signs of becoming more like trade unions [138].[1] They will, however, try to colour their behaviour so as to maintain their status in the

[1] See infra, pp. 116–18.

community. The provisions of the Industrial Relations Act 1971 will accelerate this trend, since they enable a professional association to act just like a trade union, for example, in carrying out collective bargaining, but without actually being called a union.

To function effectively professional associations will increasingly require formal contacts with each other, with trade unions in the employment situation, and with the Government as its influence increases. Such developments might provide a new stimulus for a separate white-collar TUC, although in taking such a decision professional associations would have to balance status against effectiveness.[1]

British Medical Association

The medical profession in Britain has quite a complex structure [139]. However, in numerical terms it may be viewed as having a basically two-tier structure, with the upper tier consisting of the General Medical Council which keeps a register of medical practitioners and has responsibility for standards of medical education and practice, and the lower tier consisting of the BMA which is a clear example of a protective association.[2]

The BMA seeks to advance the occupational interests of its members by direct means. It has developed into the predominant medical association as doctors have come to realize that the influence they can exert over their conditions is dependent largely on the strength and cohesion of their organization.

The internal structure of the BMA consists of local branches and divisions which send delegates to the annual representative meeting which is the governing body. Resolutions are submitted by the constituencies and those which are adopted by the representative body are implemented by the council, the executive body of the BMA [140].

Since its articles of registration as a 'company not for profit' do not allow the BMA to engage in overt trade union activities, it has established some special bodies to overcome this. The British Medical Guild was set up to collect and

[1] Supra, pp. 94–6.
[2] Supra, p. 21.

administer strike funds in case the BMA should ever advise a strike against the National Health Service; it is an organization in name only and has no members. The General Medical Services Committee represents all general practitioners in the National Health Service in negotiations over salary. It is constitutionally responsible to the Conference of Local Medical Committees, which is formally distinct from the BMA but in fact is composed of about the same people and has the same channels of influence. The other bodies for trade union activities are the Central Consultants' and Specialists' Committee, which also clings to 'the fiction of autonomy', and the Public Health Committee [141].

In these guises the BMA engages in collective bargaining and joint consultation with the Government which is effectively the employer of its members. The Whitley Councils for the Health Services are used for the discussion of the problems and grievances of individual practitioners and all aspects of general policy, for example the supply of medical materials and equipment [142]. However, this machinery is modified for questions of remuneration by having the Review Body on Doctors' and Dentists' Remuneration which makes recommendations to the Government. The BMA may then make representations to the Government on its decision following the report of the Review Body.

The BMA bargains very vigorously, and is prepared to use sanctions if necessary. In fact many observers have noted the similarities between its role and that of a trade union [143]. In 1965, for example, dissatisfaction with the award of the Review Body led to threats of resignation from the National Health Service of all BMA members in general practice, and to the fostering of the growth of a company called Independent Medical Services Ltd to organize relations between doctors and patients on a commercial basis, with an element of insurance. In 1970 the BMA instructed its members to refuse to sign sick notes in protest against the decision of the Government to refer a recommendation of the Review Body to the NBPI.

The main reason for the relatively high militancy of the BMA is that it is in a position to make such action effective.

This is because it has in its membership the majority of the members of the medical profession, the services of whom are essential for the well-being of the nation, and this position is exploited by the use of what in other occupations would be called 'restrictive practices'. The need for industrial action is accentuated by there being just a single employer for the vast majority of the membership of the BMA, making it critical that a successful influence be exerted.

Even so, the BMA is still concerned with status and attempts to justify its industrial action to the public. Thus in the 1965 dispute the association stressed that it would provide safeguards for the community, while in the 1970 dispute it claimed to be defending the independence of the Review Body. In general the BMA is careful to make known its professional aspects, which include the sponsorship of scientific activities through its board of science and education.

This balance between effectiveness and perceived status is a key factor explaining the behaviour of the BMA. Thus since the association views the medical profession as not being affected to any great degree by market pressures or trends in other industries it does not seek connections with other professional associations or with the trade union movement. Within medicine, the BMA is dominant enough to seek no connection with the MPU, particularly since this, like a connection with any union, would entail a loss in status. Politically the BMA remains a neutral body, although realizing the effect that various Government policies and agencies have on the profession, it does have 'interested members' in both Houses of Parliament.

There were signs, before the Industrial Relations Act 1971, that the BMA was becoming more like a trade union. For example, at its 1970 assembly a resolution was passed stating that 'the cardinal function of the BMA is the negotiation of satisfactory terms and conditions of service for its members' [144]. Pressure for this increasing militancy has been coming from within, and it seemed that failure of the BMA to adapt might lead to further defections following the Junior Hospital Doctors' Association, which became a section of the MPU which itself has transferred its engagements to ASTMS. The decision of the BMA to be included on the special register established under the Industrial Relations Act 1971 allows it to function in the same way as a trade union.[1] This will enable it to compete on an even footing with trade unions in the field, and even to gain an advantage if those unions do not register, and so will ensure the continuance of the BMA as the dominant medical organization.

Engineering and Scientific Bodies

The major engineering institutions, e.g. Institution of Civil Engineers, are predominantly study associations all seeking to advance the learning and the standards of the various specialist branches of engineering, and with it their status. In 1965 they formed the Council of Engineering Institutions as a central body.

It is partly because their Royal Charters have prevented the institutions from exercising a fuller function that the Engineers' Guild was established to carry out protective activities. This accepts into membership corporate members of any of the recognized engineering institutions, and it aims 'to promote and maintain the unity, public usefulness, honour and interests of the engineering profession . . .' [145]. The methods it uses includes carrying out salary surveys, which it sees of value to both employers and engineers, trying to ensure that qualified engineers are employed only in positions where their skills are fully utilized, and offering help and advice to individual members. It does not engage in collective bargaining.

The reasons for the behaviour of the Engineers' Guild are partly ideological. It typically recognizes no conflict of interest between its members and their employers, and indeed a survey taken among members of the Guild found that over half the respondents opposed collective bargaining on the grounds that it was inappropriate to their professional standing, that it would lower their status, and that it was not practicable. Of those who did support collective bargaining, over a half had reservations and thought that it should be confined to setting minimum standards or to the public sector [146]. Nevertheless, there has

[1] Supra, p. 112.

in recent years been a heightened realization in the Engineers'
Guild that status cannot be pursued exclusively, and that other
factors, and in particular the level of remuneration that members
of a profession can command, are important in themselves and
also reflect back on status. Along with this have come attempts
to engage in collective bargaining as the most effective means of
improving remuneration, but on two occasions the Guild's
claim for recognition as the appropriate negotiating body were
unsuccessful [147].

Thus a second reason why the Guild does not engage in
collective bargaining is because of lack of opportunity resulting
from low membership density. This also precludes the Guild
from taking any effective industrial action, particularly since
the membership is spread over many different organizations in
both the public and private sectors. In fact low membership
has been both a cause and an effect of the Engineers' Guild
being unsuccessful in furthering its members' interests.

The isolation of the Guild also contributes to its lack of
success. Lack of formal channels of communication with the
Government or any political party means that the Guild is
unable to express an opinion on general legislation affecting its
members, while isolation from other professional associations
and trade unions in the workplace militates against co-operation
with them on matters of common interest. The reason for the
isolation of the Engineers' Guild is to give it an appearance of
independence and therefore of high status, but in the absence
of effectiveness this becomes an irrelevance.

A consequence of the ineffectiveness of the Engineers' Guild
as a protective association is that some engineers are joining
white-collar unions, e.g. ASTMS. In an attempt to offset this
trend professional engineers are attempting to establish their
own exclusive, but effective, bargaining agent. This involves
replacing the Engineers' Guild by the Professional Engineers
Association Ltd, which will give advice to individual members
on legal points, benefit schemes and recruitment; and establishing UKAPE, a registered trade union. This body promises to
behave in a similar manner to the BMA and it has launched a
fighting fund. However the difficulty for UKAPE is to gain

recognition from the many different employers and it has already encountered difficulties [148]. The Industrial Relations Act 1971 may to some extent help UKAPE to gain recognition though this will depend on the amount of support which it can establish. Then the extent to which it will be effective will depend on the connections it can build up with the Government and with unions which view UKAPE with suspicion, and on the extent to which it is willing and able to employ sanctions to further its claims.

Each branch of science has its own separate professional association taking into membership practitioners of that science wherever they are employed, e.g. Institute of Physics, Royal Institute of Chemistry. In addition there are a number of specialist bodies which claim to be both professional associations and trade unions. Some of these have membership confined to one profession, e.g. BAC, while others have a mixed membership covering several specialisms of science and perhaps other professions as well, e.g. IPCS.

Typical aims of professional associations in science are illustrated by the Institution of Metallurgists which seeks 'To promote in every possible way the interests of and to maintain and enhance the status and prestige of metallurgists' [149]. Methods used in pursuit of these aims include carrying out salary surveys to correlate age, occupation and grade with salary, operating an appointments' register which advertises only posts with approved salaries and conditions, and giving advice to individual members on employment matters. Typically these professional associations do not negotiate salaries on behalf of members, although the Royal Institute of Chemistry claims that through informal discussions with employers and through co-operation with bodies representing the staff side in established negotiating machinery it can exert an influence over the salaries and conditions of service of members [150].

Thus these professional associations are relying on the reasonableness of employers to implement any legitimate points that they may raise. They have no recourse to sanctions, seeing these as unnecessary and not in keeping with their status ideology, nor do they have many connections with outside bodies. It is not surprising, therefore, that they are rather in-effective organizations for protecting the employment interests of their members.

The weakness of the professional associations is a factor giving impetus to membership of the other bodies. However, BAC is caught in a vicious circle of low membership and ineffectiveness. It does not conduct formal negotiations, but publishes minimum salary scales and takes up the cases of individual members. IPCS, on the other hand, has been able to serve its members fairly well, but only because of the favourable attitudes towards white-collar unionism existing in the Civil Service. Its primary concern is with the remuneration of its members, and it collects and analyses data in connection with salary claims. However, the IPCS sees its function not so much as that of challenging the system, but rather of making it work more efficiently by providing for the representation of staff opinions and reactions [151]. By registering as a trade union under the Industrial Relations Act 1971, IPCS should be able to function more effectively in the future.

The rapid growth of white-collar unions, and in particular ASTMS, in recent years is viewed as a threat by the above bodies. If they are to survive they will have to be prepared to be more militant and to engage in collective bargaining, since status cannot be defended in isolation from material well-being. It is in response to this challenge that five professional associa-tions in science, the Royal Institute of Chemistry and the Institutes of Physics, Mathematics, Biology and Metallurgy, have established the Association of Professional Scientists and Technologists. This will register as a trade union and seek to use the provisions of the Industrial Relations Act 1971 to gain recognition as a bargaining agent. The attraction to professional scientists of having their own protective body rather than being numerically submerged in more general unions is fairly sub-stantial, but ultimately the survival of the Association of Professional Scientists and Technologists will rest on its effectiveness as a bargaining agent.

5 · Conclusions

This study has given a broad survey of the present position of white-collar unionism in Britain. The system described here is a dynamic one, and the text is current at January 1972, apart from a number of more recent insertions. Unavoidably, membership statistics refer to earlier dates than this.

A general picture of the size and distribution of the white-collar labour force and of the organizations of white-collar unionism was obtained. It was found that about 50 per cent of white-collar employees are members of either a trade union, a staff association or a professional association, which is a similar figure to the density of union membership among blue-collar employees. The growth in the membership of unions by white-collar employees was found to be taking place at a greater rate than the expansion of the white-collar labour force.

However, two major difficulties were encountered in examining the extent of white-collar unionism. One of these is the absence, except for trade unions in manufacturing industries, of information on the occupational and industrial breakdown of the membership of white-collar unionism. The other is the lack of an objective and quantifiable measure of the nature of unionism. A possible long-term solution to problems of the first type would be the establishment of a national pool of raw data from which researchers could extract the statistics they require. (The CODOT system, recently announced by the DE, could provide a basis for such a data pool.) The second difficulty points to a specific research need.

The study examined only the main factors affecting white-collar unionism, and discounted possible secondary factors such as the age distribution of employees or the public image of the trade union movement because of lack of evidence of their effect. It was found that the most significant factors affecting the membership of white-collar unionism are the work environment, particularly the degree of employment concentration, and the attitude of employers and the Government, particularly over the recognition of unions. Social status was found to be the most significant factor affecting the nature of unionism. The employment of women was found to have an indirect effect on white-collar unionism as a result of their typical employment situation. Other factors such as the level of employment, technical change, takeovers and mergers, and pay and fringe benefits were found only to have a general background influence and not to determine differences in the membership and nature of unionism between groups of white-collar employees. It was predicted that trends in the various factors will, on balance, lead to a future increase both in the overall membership density of white-collar unionism and in the vigour with which these organizations act.

This section of the book indicated several areas where further research is needed. One of these is a rigorous examination of the effects of the level of employment on white-collar unionism. Another is a fuller investigation of the effects of factors such as the level of pay and the work environment on the membership of staff associations and professional associations.

In its discussion of the characteristics of white-collar unionism, the study examined not only the structure, activities and relations of the various organizations but also, where possible, the reasons for these. Predictions were also made of the likely future trends in the various characteristics.

Trade unions were found to have an overlapping structural pattern but to be taking some steps to try to co-ordinate their activities. In their internal organizations a fairly general trend towards basing branches on the workplace and providing separate representation for special interest groups was discovered. It was found that unions for white-collar employees are affiliating to the TUC in increasing numbers because of the instrumental advantages to be gained, but the stand taken by the TUC on registration under the Industrial Relations Act

1971 may slow this trend. However, it seems likely that there will remain just one central body for the trade union movement in Britain. It was also predicted that in the future more unions will engage in political activities, again for instrumental reasons. In their relations with employers, unions for white-collar employees were seen to be increasingly involved in managerial as well as market relations and to be more willing to engage in industrial action. It was predicted that if the provisions of the Industrial Relations Act 1971 are fully used, and the indications at the moment are that they will not be, then they will introduce an inflexibility into the relations between unions and employers, and have a mixed effect on membership participation.

Two areas where further research would be useful were revealed by this section of the study. These are an investigation into the effect on managers of holding part-time union office, and an analysis of the benefits to a union of administering certain welfare and educational services.

Staff associations in general were found to be dependent upon employers, to be isolated from each other and from trade unions and professional associations, and to offer few welfare benefits to their members. It was predicted that staff associations operating in areas where unions register under the Industrial Relations Act are likely to decline while those operating in other areas may well become a little more independent and build up their membership. Bank staff associations were found to have grown increasingly independent over the years, and a long-term trend towards a single registered union in banking was predicted.

A difficulty encountered in examining staff associations was the shortage of published material outside of banking, and there is a need for further research in this field.

The study found that professional associations are independent bodies which lay great emphasis on enhancing the status of their profession. They remain largely isolated from each other and from trade unions, staff associations and political parties. It was found that many of them use only indirect methods such as salary surveys to try to further the interests of their members, while others, e.g. BMA, engage in collective bargaining and use sanctions against the employer. It was predicted that, in order to remain effective, all professional associations will have to give more emphasis to collective bargaining, and will seek industrial, and perhaps also political, affiliations. In so doing they will take advantage of provisions in the Industrial Relations Act.

Overall, the survey has revealed the size and scope of white-collar unionism in Britain, and has given insights into the great changes which are taking place. The impact of white-collar unionism on the current and future pattern of industrial relations cannot be overemphasized.

Appendix 1 · White-Collar Unions Affiliated to the TUC

Name	Membership (31-12-70)	% change in membership from 1964 to 1970
ABS	11,235	+8·5
ABT	2,125	+6·2
ACTT	16,545	+40·0
AGSRO	10,777	+3·1 (1)
APECCS	125,541	+58·0
APOE	14,187	+18·0 (1)
ASTMS	220,600	+296·0 (4)
ATTI	29,740	+16·0 (2)
BALPA	4,005	+42·0
CCOA	5,151	+9·0 (2)
CEF	4,300	+22·0
CEPSA	2,845	+3·6 (3)
CPSA	184,935	+26·0
EPEA	29,612	+31·0
Equity	17,983	+17·0 (5)
ESA	2,194	+3·9
FAA	2,175	−7·2
GLCSA	14,096	+30·0
GUALO	3,920	−18·0
HVA	5,432	+26·0
IRSF	49,735	+22·0
MLSA	15,899	+36·0
MNALOA	21,000	+15·0
MOS	1,997	+4·0
MPU	5,502	−2·5
MU	32,892	−7·6

	(31-12-70)	from 1964 to 1970
NALGO	439,887	+30·0
NAS	56,899	+36·0 (1)
NATKE	15,643	−24·0
NUBE	89,144	+58·0
NUCO	6,742	−22·0
NUIW	35,928	−6·0
NUJ	24,503	+36·0
NUT	310,536	+44·0
PFTA	2,160	0·0
POA	13,658	+32·0 (2)
POMSA	17,109	+20·0
RBSATEA	3,584	+13·0
REOU	2,963	−15·0
STCS	9,332	−4·7
SUPLO	500	0·0
TASS	105,418	+6·0
TSSA	75,194	−4·7
WGGB	1,656	+6·0
YAPLO	1,808	+1·3
Total	2,046,187	+75·0 (6)

Notes: (1) From 1968–70. (2) From 1966–70. (3) From 1965–70. (4) Calculated using total membership of ASSET and AScW at 31/12/64. (5) Calculated using total membership of Equity and Variety Artistes' Federation at 31/12/64. (6) Calculated using total membership of white-collar unions affiliated to TUC at 31/12/64.

Sources: Membership figures from Statistical Statement in *TUC Report 1971*, % change in membership calculated using Statistical Statement in *TUC Report 1965, 1966, 1968*. NUT figure direct from union.

Appendix 2 · Principal Partially White-Collar Unions Affiliated to the TUC

Name	Membership at 31-12-70 Total	Membership at 31-12-70 White-collar (1)	% change in membership 1964–1970 Total	% change in membership 1964–1970 White-collar	Main white-collar grades organized
AUEW	1,267,218	7,200 (2)	+17·0	+900·0	Supervisors, technicians, rate fixers, draughtsmen, planning engineers, producers of tape controls
CHSE	89,550	59,000	+40·0	+48·0	Professional, technical, administrative and clerical staff
CSU	35,247	29,000	+36·0	+78·0	Instructional officers, telephonists, office keepers, coast guards, museum grades
EETU-PTU	420,588	11,300 (3)	+25·0	+400·0	Supervisors, technicians, some clerical workers in electrical industry
FBU	30,000	1,000 (4)	+24	–	
GMWU	853,353	26,000 (5)	+8·8	+110·0	Supervisory, professional, scientific, technical, clerical and administrative workers
ISTC	116,632	19,000	+2·0	+110·0	Clerical, technical, administrative and supervisory staff up to middle management grades
NACODS	23,389	21,500	–30·0	–19·0	Supervisors below ground in the mining industry
NGA	107,360	2,700 (4)	+27·0	–	Press telegraphists and correctors
NUM	279,453	16,600 (6)	–42·0	–21·0	Clerical and junior administrative staff
NUPE	372,709	78,500	+55·0	+160·0	Administrative, technical, clerical and professional employees in public authorities, e.g. nurses, laboratory assistants

Name	Membership at 31-12-70		% change in membership 1964-1970		Main white-collar grades organized
	Total	White-collar (1)	Total	White-collar	
NUR	198,319	10,000	−25·0	0·0	Clerical and supervisory staff
POEU	116,559	26,500	+34·0	+33·0	Supervisors, technicians, some office managers
SOGAT (7)	243,901	17,600	+12·0	+24·0	Representatives; clerical and administrative grades
TGWU	1,638,686	83,000	+15·0	+47·0	Clerks, supervisors, administrators, technicians
UPW	209,479	64,800	+15·0	+190·0	Telegraph operators, radio operators, telegraphists, telephonists
USDAW	329,890	260,000 (4)	−6·3	–	Clerks, supervisors, shop assistants in wholesale and retail distributive trades, insurance agents, dental technicians
Total	6,332,333	733,700	+9·1	+34·5	

Notes:

(1) Approximate numbers.
(2) Supervisory branch membership only, excluding TASS.
(3) Technical and Supervisory Section membership only.
(4) Estimated from Bain (1967), op. cit., Appendix A.
(5) Affiliation figure to TUC Non-Manual Workers' Conference.
(6) Excludes supervisory industrial staff.
(7) The amalgamation of NATSOPA and NUPBPW. In 1970, NATSOPA broke away from SOGAT.

Source : Total membership from Statistical Statement in *TUC Report 1971.*
White-collar membership estimated from figures obtained direct from individual unions.
% change in total membership calculated using Statistical Statement in *TUC Report 1965.*
% change in white-collar membership calculated using G. S. Bain, *Trade Union Growth and Recognition,* Research Paper 6 of the Royal Commission on Trade Unions and Employers' Associations (London, HMSO, 1967), Appendix A.

E

Appendix 3 · Principal Non-TUC Affliated White-Collar Unions, Staff Associations and Professional Associations

Name	Membership (1970)	Classification	Notes
Association of Local Government Engineers and Surveyors	3,000	Trade Union	Probably considerable dual membership with NALGO
Association of University Teachers	17,526	Professional Association	
Bank Staff Associations	75,000 (1)	Staff Associations	
British Association of Chemists	1,600	Trade Union	Claims to be also a professional association
British Association of Colliery Management	16,000	Trade Union	Has 95% membership density
British Dental Association	10,000	Professional Association	Has 80% membership density
British Legal Association	2,700	Professional Association	
British Medical Association	66,725 (2)	Professional Association	Has 80% membership density
British Transport Officers' Guild	2,600 (3)	Trade Union	
Engineers' Guild	7,200	Professional Association	Has 5% membership density
Incorporated Association of Assistant Masters in Secondary Schools	30,000	Trade Union	
Institution of Metallurgists	10,000	Professional Association	
Institute of Physics	15,000	Professional Association	Objects: Advancement of knowledge of physics, pure and applied; and elevation of profession of physicist
Institution of Professional Civil Servants	85,000	Trade Union	Objects: Promotion of interests and professional knowledge of members, and advancement of efficiency of HM Civil Service

Name	Membership (1970)	Classification	Notes
Institution of Water Engineers	3,000	Trade Union	
Law Society	19,600	Professional Association	
Royal College of Nursing	45,000	Professional Association	
Royal Institute of British Architects	23,000	Professional Association	
Royal Institute of Chemistry	23,000	Professional Association	Aims: Promotion of profession, as distinct from science, of chemistry; and furtherance of interests of qualified chemists
United Kingdom Association of Professional Engineers	9,000	Trade Union	
Total	464,950		

Notes:
(1) At December 1964.
(2) At March 1969.
(3) At 1969.

Source: Membership figures from Directory of British Associations – Edition 3, 1971–2 (Beckenham, CBD Research Ltd), except for Bank Staff Associations from R. M. Blackburn, Union Character and Social Class (London, Batsford, 1967), p. 79; BMA, BTOG and The Law Society, direct from these associations; and UKAPE from the Sunday Times 16 August 1970.

Appendix 4 · Composition of the TUC General Council

No.	Trade Group Name	White-collar unions Names	White-collar unions Membership (31-12-70)	Partially white-collar unions Names	Partially white-collar unions White-collar membership (31-12-70)	Total membership (31-12-70) White-collar	Total membership (31-12-70) All	Representation on General Council (1971-72) From white-collar unions	Representation on General Council (1971-72) From partially white-collar unions	Representation on General Council (1971-72) Total
1.	Mining and Quarrying	–	–	NACODS NUM	38,100	38,100	302,842	–	2	2
2.	Railways	TSSA	75,194	NUR	10,000	85,194	302,790	1	1	2
3.	Transport (other than railways)	BALPA MNALOA REOU	27,968	TGWU	83,000	110,968	1,761,998	–	4	5
4.	Shipbuilding	–	–	–	–	–	127,285	–	1	1
5.	Engineering, Founding, and Vehicle Building	–	–	AUEW	7,200	7,200	1,539,995	–	3	4
6.	Technical, Engineering and Scientific	ABT TASS EPEA ESA ASTMS	359,949	–	–	359,949	359,949	1	–	1
7.	Electricity	–	–	EETU-PTU	11,300	11,300	420,588	–	1	1
8.	Iron and Steel, and Minor Metal Trades	–	–	ISTC	19,000	19,000	158,432	–	1	1

Trade group		White-collar unions		Partially white-collar unions		Total membership (31-12-70)		Representation on General Council (1971-72)		
No.	Name	Names	Membership (31-12-70)	Names	White-collar membership (31-12-70)	White-collar	All	From white-collar unions	From partially white-collar unions	Total
9.	Building, Wood-working and Furnishing	–	–	–	–	–	375,628	–	–	2
10.	Printing and Paper	NUJ	24,503	SOGAT NGA	20,300	44,803	403,199	–	1	1
11.	Textiles	GUALO MOS SUPLO YAPLO	8,225	–	–	8,225	149,173	–	–	1
12.	Clothing, Leather and Boot and Shoe	–	–	–	–	–	268,866	–	–	1
13.	Glass, Ceramics, Chemicals, Food, Drink, Tobacco, Brushmaking and Distribution	NUCO RBSATEA	10,326	CWU USDAW TWU	260,500	270,826	476,269	–	1	2
14.	Agriculture	–	–	–	–	–	100,000	–	–	1
15.	Public Employees	GLCSA HVA MPU NALGO ATTI NAS NUT	862,092	FBU CHSE NUPE	138,500	1,000,592	1,358,403	3	2	5

Trade group		White-collar unions		Partially white-collar unions		Total membership (31-12-70)		Representation on General Council (1971-72)		
No.	Name	Names	Membership (31-12-70)	Names	White-collar membership (31-12-70)	White-collar	All	From white-collar unions	From partially white-collar unions	Total
16. Civil Servants		CPSA CCOA CEF CEPSA IRSF AGSRO MLSA POMSA POA STCS APOE	327,928	CSU POEU UPW	120,300	448,228	689,213	1	1	2
17. Professional, Clerical and Entertainment		Equity NUBE ABS ACTT APECCS FAA NUIW MU PFTA NATKE WGGB	350,002	–	–	350,002	350,002	2	–	2

No.	Name	White-collar unions Names	Membership (31-12-70)	Partially white-collar unions Names	White-collar membership (31-12-70)	Total membership (31-12-70) White-collar	All	Representation on General Council (1971-72) From white-collar unions	From partially white-collar unions	Total
18.	General Workers	—	—	GMWU	26,000	26,000	857,572	—	3	3
	Total		2,046,187		734,200	2,780,387	10,002,204	8	20	37

Source: Statistical Statement in *TUC Report 1971*, and direct from partially white-collar unions.

Appendix 5 · List of Reference Works

BOOKS AND ARTICLES

V. L. ALLEN, *Power in Trade Unions*, London, Longmans, 1954.

V. L. ALLEN, *Trade Unions and the Government*, London, Longmans, 1960.

G. S. BAIN, *Trade Union Growth and Recognition* (Research Paper 6 of the Royal Commission on Trade Unions and Employers' Associations), London, HMSO, 1967.

G. S. BAIN, *The Growth of White-Collar Unionism*, London, Oxford University Press, 1970.

G. S. BAIN and R. PRICE, 'Union Growth and Employment Trends in the U.K., 1964–70', *BJIR*, November 1972.

R. M. BLACKBURN, *Union Character and Social Class*, London, Batsford, 1967.

V. BURKE, *Teachers in Turmoil*, Harmondsworth, Penguin, 1971.

A. M. CARR-SAUNDERS and P. A. WILSON, *The Professions*, London, Frank Cass, 1964.

H. A. CLEGG, A. J. KILLICK and R. ADAMS, *Trade Union Officers*, Oxford, Blackwell, 1961.

J. R. DALE, *The Clerk in Industry*, Liverpool, Liverpool University Press, 1962.

B. DONOUGHUE, 'Trade Unions in a Changing Society', *Planning*, Vol. XXIX, No. 472, PEP, 1963.

H. M. DOUTY, 'Salary Determination for White-Collar Civil Servants in Great Britain', *Monthly Labour Review*, November 1960.

H. ECKSTEIN, *Pressure Group Politics*, London, Allen & Unwin, 1960.

A. FLANDERS, *Industrial Relations : What is Wrong with the System*, London, Faber & Faber, 1965.

A. FLANDERS, *Trade Unions*, London, Hutchinson, 1968.

A. FLANDERS, 'Collective Bargaining: A Theoretical Analysis', *BJIR*, March 1968.

A. FOX, *Industrial Sociology and Industrial Relations* (Research Paper 3 of the Royal Commission on Trade Unions and Employers' Associations), London, HMSO, 1966.

D. V. GLASS (ed.), *Social Mobility in Britain*, London, Routledge & Kegan Paul, 1954.

B. GOLDSTEIN, 'Some Aspects of the Nature of Unionism among Salaried Professionals in Industry', *American Sociological Review*, Vol. 20, 1955.

J. H. GOLDTHORPE, D. LOCKWOOD, F. BECHHOFER and J. PLATT, *The Affluent Worker in the Class Structure*, Cambridge, Cambridge University Press, 1969.

D. S. HAMERMESH, 'Professional and White-Collar Unionism', *Industrial Relations*, October 1966.

M. HARRISON, *Trade Unions and the Labour Party since 1945*, London, Allen & Unwin, 1960.

K. HINDELL, 'Trade Union Membership', *Planning*, Vol. XXVIII, No. 463, PEP, 1962.

J. HUGHES, *Trade Union Structure and Government* (Research Paper 5 (Parts 1 and 2) of the Royal Commission on Trade Unions' and Employers' Associations), London, HMSO, 1967 and 1968.

C. JENKINS and J. E. MORTIMER, *The Kind of Laws the Unions Ought to Want*, Oxford, Pergamon, 1968.

R. K. KELSALL and H. M. KELSALL, *The School Teacher in England and the United States*, Oxford, Pergamon, 1969.

V. KLEIN, 'Working Wives', *IPM Occasional Paper*, No. 15, 1959.

A. KLEINGARTNER, *Professionalism and Salaried Worker Organization*, Madison, Wis., University of Wisconsin, 1967.

S. B. LEVINE, 'The White-Collar, Blue-Collar Alliance in Japan', Symposium, *Industrial Relations*, October 1965.

D. LOCKWOOD, *The Blackcoated Worker*, London, Allen & Unwin, 1958.

R. A. MANZER, *Teachers and Politics*, Manchester, Manchester University Press, 1970.

C. J. MARGERISON and C. K. ELLIOTT, 'A Predictive Study in the Development in Teacher Militancy', *BJIR*, November 1970.

R. M. MARTIN, 'Australian Professional and White-Collar Unions', Symposium, *Industrial Relations*, October 1965.

B. MCCORMICK, 'Managerial Unionism in the Coal Industry', *British Journal of Sociology*, Vol. 11, 1960.

C. WRIGHT MILLS, *White-Collar: American Middle Classes*, New York, Oxford University Press, 1956.

E. MUMFORD and O. BANKS, *The Computer and the Clerk*, London, Routledge & Kegan Paul, 1967.

G. E. C. PATON, 'Managerial Trade Unionism in Britain', *Scientific Business*, November 1964.

K. PRANDY, *Professional Employees*, London, Faber & Faber, 1965.

K. PRANDY, 'Professional Organizations in Great Britain', Symposium, *Industrial Relations*, October 1965.

B. C. ROBERTS, G. ROUTH, N. SEEAR, W. PICKLES and S. LERNER, *Industrial Relations – Contemporary Problems and Perspectives*, London, Methuen, 1968.

O. ROBINSON, 'Representation of the White-Collar Worker: The Bank Staff Associations in Britain', *BJIR*, March 1969.

W. ROY, 'Membership Participation in the National Union of Teachers', *BJIR*, July 1964.

D. SCHON, 'The Loss of the Stable State' (1970 Reith Lectures), *The Listener*, 19 November 1970.

A. STURMTHAL, G. ROUTH, E. M. KASSALOW and S. B. LEVINE, *White-Collar Trade Unions*, Urbana, Ill., University of Illinois Press, 1967.

A. J. M. SYKES, 'Some Differences in the Attitudes of Clerical and Manual Workers', *Sociological Review*, XIII, November 1965.

H. A. TURNER, *Trade Union Growth, Structure and Policy*, London, Allen & Unwin, 1962.

H. A. TURNER, 'The Royal Commission's Research Papers', *BJIR*, November 1968.

D. VOLKER, 'NALGO's Affiliation to the TUC', *BJIR*, March 1966.

K. W. WEDDERBURN, *The Worker and the Law* (2nd edition), Harmondsworth, Penguin Books, 1971.

MINUTES, REPORTS ETC.

ABC of the TUC, London, TUC, 1969.

The Case for the British Manager, London, ASTMS, 1969.

Department of Employment Gazette. Formerly *Employment and Productivity Gazette* (various).

Directory of British Associations – Edition 2, 1967–8, Beckenham, CBD Research Ltd.

Industrial Relations: Programme for Action, London, TUC, 1969.

Industrial Relations Bill (Bill 164), London, HMSO, 1970.

Industrial Relations Act 1971.

Industrial Relations Handbook, London, HMSO, 1961.

In Place of Strife: A Policy for Industrial Relations (Cmnd. 3888), London, HMSO, 1969.

Management Succession, London, Acton Society Trust, 1956.

Manpower Studies No. 4 – Computers in Offices, Ministry of Labour Manpower Research Unit, London, HMSO, 1965.

Minutes of Evidence of Association of Supervisory Staffs, Executives and Technicians to Royal Commission on Trade Unions and Employers' Associations, London, HMSO, 1967.

Minutes of Evidence of Confederation of British Industry to Royal Commission on Trade Unions and Employers' Associations, London, HMSO, 1966.

Minutes of Evidence of Draughtsmen's and Allied Technicians' Association to Royal Commission on Trade Unions and Employers' Associations, London, HMSO, 1967.

Minutes of Evidence of National and Local Government Officers' Association to Royal Commission on Trade Unions and Employers' Associations, London, HMSO, 1966.

Minutes of Evidence of National Federation of Professional Workers to the Royal Commission on Trade Unions and Employers' Associations, London, HMSO, 1966.

Non-Manual Workers: Conference Report 1969, London, TUC, 1969.

Report of the Chief Registrar of Friendly Societies for the Years 1969 and 1970, London, HMSO, 1970 and 1971.

Report of the Inquiry by the Honourable Lord Cameron, DSC, QC, into the complaint made by the National Union of Bank Employees on 12th March 1962, to the Committee on Freedom of Association of the International Labour Organization, London, HMSO, 1963.

Report of the Royal Commission on Trade Unions and Employers' Associations (Cmnd. 3623), London, HMSO, 1968.

Staff Relations in the Civil Service, London, HMSO, 1958.

Strategy for Pensions: The future development of State and Occupational Provision (Cmnd. 4755), London, HMSO, 1971.

Teacher Education and Training, London, HMSO, 1972.

Trade Unionism, London, TUC, 1966.

TUC Reports (various).

TUC Structure and Development, London, TUC, 1970.

Union Reorganization, Esher, GMWU, 1969.

Written Evidence of NALGO to the Royal Commission on Trade Unions and Employers' Associations, London, NALGO, 1965.

You and the ATTI, London, ATTI, August 1969.

References

CHAPTER 2

[1] G. S. Bain and R. Price, 'Union Growth and Employment Trends in the U.K., 1964–70', *British Journal of Industrial Relations (BJIR)*, November 1972, pp. 368–9, Table 1. This breakdown is based for 1966.

[2] 'Occupations of Employees in Manufacturing Industries (May 1968)', *Employment and Productivity Gazette*, January 1969, pp. 14–40.

[3] Bain and Price, op. cit., pp. 368–9, Table 1.

[4] Ibid., p. 370, Table 2.

[5] Ibid., pp. 368–70, Tables 1 and 3.

[6] V. Klein, 'Working Wives', *Institute of Personnel Management (IPM) Occasional Paper*, No. 15, 1959.

[7] G. Routh, 'Trade Union Membership', in B. C. Roberts (ed.), *Industrial Relations – Contemporary Problems and Perspectives* (London, Methuen, 1968), p. 50. Figures are for 965.

[8] Bain and Price, op. cit., pp. 374–5, Table 7. Figure is for 1968.

[9] Ibid., p. 370, Table 3; figure for 1966.

[10] Ibid., pp. 368–70, Tables 1 and 3; figure for 1966.

[11] R. M. Blackburn, *Union Character and Social Class* (London, Batsford, 1967), p. 14.

[12] Industrial Relations Act 1971, s. 61(3).

[13] *Minutes of Evidence of National and Local Government Officers' Association (NALGO) to the Royal Commission on Trade Unions and Employers' Associations* (London, HMSO, 1966), p. 1039, q. 3921.

[14] See, for example, A. Kleingartner, *Professionalism and Salaried Worker Organization* (Madison, Wis., University of Wisconsin, 1967), pp. 4–17; and A. M. Carr-Saunders and P. A. Wilson, *The Professions* (London, Frank Cass, 1964), p. 284.

[15] From G. Millerson, *The Qualifying Associations* (London, Routledge & Kegan Paul, 1964); cited in Blackburn, op. cit., pp. 22–3.

[16] Blackburn, op. cit., pp. 18–19.

[17] G. S. Bain, *Trade Union Growth and Recognition*, Research Paper 6 of the Royal Commission on Trade Unions and Employers' Associations (London, HMSO, 1967), p. 17. Figures are for 1964.

[18] H. A. Turner, 'The Royal Commission's Research Papers', *BJIR*, November 1968, p. 354.

[19] Ibid.

[20] Bain, op. cit., p. 17, Table 11; and Bain and Price, op. cit., p. 378, Table 10.

[21] Bain, op. cit., p. 25, Table 15.

[22] Ibid., p. 27, Table 16. Figures are for 1964.

[23] K. Prandy, *Professional Employees* (London, Faber & Faber, 1965), p. 130.

[24] G. E. C. Paton, 'Managerial Trade Unionism in Britain', *Scientific Business*, November 1964, p. 265, Tables 1 and 2.

[25] J. Hughes, *Trade Union Structure and Government*, Research Paper 5 (Part 2) of the Royal Commission on Trade Unions and Employers' Associations (London, HMSO, 1968), pp. 28–9.

[26] G. S. Bain, *The Growth of White-Collar Unionism* (London, Oxford University Press, 1970), pp. 37–8.

CHAPTER 3

[1] D. Lockwood, *The Blackcoated Worker* (London, Allen & Unwin, 1958), pp. 106–7.

[2] Ibid., pp. 112–13. This figure is derived from the enquiry described in D. V. Glass (ed.), *Social Mobility in Britain* (London, Routledge & Kegan Paul, 1954), Chapter IV.

[3] E. Mumford and O. Banks, *The Computer and the Clerk* (London, Routledge & Kegan Paul, 1967), p. 66.

[4] See G. Routh, 'White-Collar Unions in the United Kingdom', in A. Sturmthal (ed.), *White-Collar Trade Unions* (Urbana, Ill., University of Illinois Press, 1967), p. 168.

[5] See, for example, D. Lockwood, op. cit., pp. 125–30.

[6] See, for example, B. Donoughue, 'Trade Unions in a Changing Society', *Planning*, Vol. XXIX, No. 472, Political and Economic Planning (PEP), 1963, p. 203. The extent of this breakdown should not be overemphasized, however; see J. H. Goldthorpe,

D. Lockwood, F. Bechhofer and J. Platt, *The Affluent Worker in the Class Structure* (Cambridge, Cambridge University Press, 1969).

[7] An example is teaching. See C. J. Margerison and C. K. Elliott, 'A Predictive Study in the Development in Teacher Militancy', *BJIR*, November 1970, p. 411.

[8] Clerks are an example. See J. R. Dale, *The Clerk in Industry* (Liverpool, Liverpool University Press, 1962), Chapter 3.

[9] C. W. Mills, *White-Collar: American Middle Classes* (New York, Oxford University Press, 1956), pp. 306–7 and 312.

[10] G. S. Bain, *The Growth of White-Collar Unionism* (London, Oxford University Press, 1970), pp. 43–6 and 48–50.

[11] R. M. Blackburn, *Union Character and Social Class* (London, Batsford, 1967), pp. 198–9.

[12] K. Prandy, *Professional Employees* (London, Faber & Faber, 1965), Chapter 8. This provides a study of qualified members of the Association of Scientific Workers, which is now amalgamated into ASTMS.

[13] Ibid., Chapter 6.

[14] Ibid.

[15] See, for example, V. Burke, *Teachers in Turmoil* (Harmondsworth, Penguin, 1971), pp. 29–40.

[16] Margerison and Elliott, op. cit., pp. 415–16.

[17] Mills, op. cit., p. 308.

[18] Figures from *The Observer*, 23 August 1970.

[19] Prandy, op. cit., Chapter 6.

[20] Margerison and Elliott, op. cit., pp. 414–15.

[21] Bain, op. cit., pp. 41–3.

[22] A typical example is banking. See Blackburn, op. cit., pp. 71–4.

[23] See J. Hughes, *Trade Union Structure and Government*, Research Paper 5 (Part 2) of the Royal Commission on Trade Unions and Employers' Associations (London, HMSO, 1968), p. 18.

[24] Ibid., pp. 20–1.

[25] For example, see Blackburn, op. cit., p. 121.

[26] Lockwood, op. cit., p. 152.

[27] N. Seear, 'Relationships at Factory Level', in B. C. Roberts (ed.), *Industrial Relations – Contemporary Problems and Perspectives* (London, Methuen, 1968), p. 174.

[28] K. Hindell, 'Trade Union Membership', *Planning*, Vol. XXVIII, No. 463, PEP, 1962, pp. 167–8.

[29] Hughes, op. cit., pp. 28–9.

[30] *Trade Unionism* (London, TUC, 1966), p. 131.

[31] *Department of Employment Gazette*, December 1971, pp. 1179 and 1184. Unemployment figure at November 1971.

[32] Ibid., November 1971, pp. 1048–53.

[33] Hindell, op. cit., pp. 161–3.

[34] A. Sturmthal, 'A Comparative Essay', in Sturmthal (ed.), op. cit., p. 391.

[35] D. Schon, 'The Loss of the Stable State' (1970 Reith Lectures), *The Listener*, 19 November 1970.

[36] Dale, op. cit., p. 88.

[37] Ministry of Labour Manpower Research Unit, *Manpower Studies No. 4 – Computers in Offices* (London, HMSO, 1965).

[38] Mumford and Banks, op. cit., p. 26.

[39] *Written Evidence of NALGO to Royal Commission on Trade Unions and Employers' Associations* (London, NALGO, 1965), p. 10.

[40] Prandy, op. cit., Chapter 8.

[41] Bain, op. cit., pp. 98–9.

[42] *Minutes of Evidence of Association of Supervisory Staffs, Executives and Technicians (ASSET) to the Royal Commission on Trade Unions and Employers' Associations* (London, HMSO, 1967), p. 2254, para. 91.

[43] Bain, op. cit., pp. 51–2.

[44] 'Has the Salariat Prospered?, I & II', *The Economist*, 23 and 30 May 1964.

[45] Ibid.

[46] *Department of Employment Gazette*, January 1972, p. 114, Table 129.

[47] Ibid.

[48] G. Routh, 'Trade Union Membership', in Roberts (ed.), op. cit., p. 39, Table 2.

[49] See, for example, Bain, op. cit., pp. 63–7.

[50] *Department of Employment Gazette*, August 1971, pp. 698–9 and 707–8, Tables 3, 4, 11 and 12.

[51] C. Jenkins and J. E. Mortimer, *The Kind of Laws the Unions Ought to Want* (London, Pergamon, 1968), pp. 143–6.

[52] *Strategy for Pensions: The Future Development of State and Occupational Provision*, Cmnd. 4755 (London, HMSO, 1971), pp. 16–17.

[53] Lockwood, op. cit., p. 150.

[54] Bain, op. cit., p. 61.

[55] Ibid., pp. 54–8 and 67.

[56] Margerison and Elliott, op. cit., pp. 412–13.

[57] *Minutes of Evidence of ASSET* . . ., pp. 2247–8. This is also an objective of white-collar unions in Australia, Austria, France, Germany. See Sturmthal, op. cit., p. 395.

[58] Prandy, op. cit., Chapter 5.

[59] *Strategy for Pensions* . . ., p. 10.

[60] Lockwood, op. cit., pp. 78–81.

[61] See, for example, Donoughue, op. cit., p. 175.

[62] *Management Succession* (London, Acton Society Trust, 1956); and Geoffrey Thomas, *Labour Mobility in Great Britain 1945–9*, p. 29, cited in Lockwood, op. cit., p. 175.

[63] Dale, op. cit., p. 53. See also Mills, op. cit., p. 309.

[64] See Routh in Roberts (ed.), op. cit., p. 38, Table 1, which shows that two-thirds of all draughtsmen are under 35; and *Minutes of Evidence of Draughtsmen's and Allied Technicians' Association (DATA) to Royal Commission on Trade Unions and Employers' Associations* (London, HMSO, 1967), pp. 1518–19, which shows that many draughtsmen are promoted.

[65] Bain, op. cit., pp. 79–80.

[66] Lockwood, op. cit., pp. 141–3; and Prandy, op. cit., pp. 160–3.

[67] Lockwood, op. cit., pp. 143–5.

[68] Blackburn, op. cit., p. 242.

[69] Prandy, op. cit., pp. 151–2.

[70] Bain, op. cit., p. 86.

[71] An example is BACM. See B. McCormick, 'Managerial Unionism in the Coal Industry', *British Journal of Sociology*, Vol. II, 1960, p. 366. There are exceptions such as ASTMS.

[72] Prandy, op. cit., Chapter 5.

[73] On this latter point, see the example of male teachers in Margerison and Elliott, op. cit., pp. 414–15.

[74] A. J. M. Sykes, 'Some Differences in the Attitudes of Clerical and Manual Workers', *Sociological Review*, XIII, November 1965, pp. 307–10.

[75] Margerison and Elliott, op. cit., pp. 414–15.

[76] A. Fox, *Industrial Sociology and Industrial Relations*, Research Paper 3 of the Royal Commission on Trade Unions and Employers' Associations (London, HMSO, 1966), pp. 4 and 6–10.

[77] G. S. Bain, *Trade Union Growth and Recognition*, Research Paper 6 of the Royal Commission on Trade Unions and Employers' Associations (London, HMSO, 1967), p. 78, para. 179.

[78] See, for example, *Staff Relations in the Civil Service* (London, HMSO, 1958), p. 3.

[79] Fox, op. cit., pp. 3–5.

[80] Ibid., pp. 10–14; and Bain (1967), op. cit., pp. 74–82.

[81] Bain (1967), op. cit., p. 73, Table 18.

[82] Ibid., p. 69.

[83] 'W & C 1947', published as Appendix to Written Memorandum of Evidence in *Minutes of Evidence of DATA . . .*, p. 1550.

[84] *Minutes of Evidence of Confederation of British Industry (CBI) to Royal Commission on Trade Unions and Employers' Associations* (London, HMSO, 1966), p. 822, q. 3339.

[85] Bain (1967), op. cit., pp. 82–5.

[86] Ibid.

[87] 'Second Written Memorandum of Evidence', in *Minutes of Evidence of ASSET . . .*, p. 2260.

[88] Blackburn, op. cit., p. 86ff.

[89] Bain (1967), op. cit., pp. 85–9.

[90] 'W & C 1947', in *Minutes of Evidence of DATA . . .*, pp. 1550–1.

[91] For this and other examples, see Bain (1970), op. cit., pp. 127–130.

[92] Bain (1967), op. cit., pp. 92–5.

[93] See 'Second Written Memorandum of Evidence', in *Minutes of Evidence of ASSET . . .*, p. 2260.

[94] 'Third Written Memorandum of Evidence', in *Minutes of Evidence of ASSET . . .*, pp. 2262–6.

[95] Bain (1967), op. cit., pp. 95–6; and *Minutes of Evidence of National Federation of Professional Workers (NFPW) to Royal Commission on Trade Unions and Employers' Associations* (London, HMSO, 1966), pp. 1071–2, paras 4105–7.

[96] Prandy, op. cit., p. 157; and a case at Goodyear Tyre and Rubber Co. Ltd in 'Second Written Memorandum of Evidence', in *Minutes of Evidence of ASSET . . .*, p. 2260.

[97] Bain (1970), op. cit., pp. 124–6.

[98] See Blackburn, op. cit., p. 200ff. For another example, see McCormick, op. cit., p. 367.

[99] *Trade Unionism . . .*, p. 112.

[100] See, for example, A. Flanders, *Industrial Relations: What is Wrong with the System?* (London, Faber & Faber, 1965), Chapter 3.

[101] For a popular discussion see K. W. Wedderburn, *The Worker and the Law*, 2nd edn (Harmondsworth, Penguin, 1971).

[102] Bain (1967), op. cit., pp. 31–62.

[103] Bain (1970), op. cit., p. 182.

[104] Bain (1967), op. cit., pp. 62–7.

[105] *Report of the Royal Commission on Trade Unions and Employers' Associations 1965–1968*, Cmnd. 3623 (London, HMSO, 1968), p. 198, para. 737.

[106] Ibid., pp. 62–4.

[107] Ibid., pp. 48–51, 68–70 and 147–9.

[108] See *In Place of Strife: A Policy for Industrial Relations*, Cmnd. 3888 (London, HMSO, 1969), pp. 18–19 and 31; and Industrial Relations Bill (Bill 164) (London, HMSO, 1970), ss. 6–15, 36, 57.

[109] Industrial Relations Act 1971, ss. 5, 22 and 106.

[110] Ibid., ss. 44–53.

[111] See E. M. Kassalow, 'White-Collar Unionism in the United States', in Sturmthal (ed.), op. cit., pp. 331–3.

[112] *Report of the Royal Commission . . .*, p. 83, para. 322; and *In Place of Strife . . .*, p. 12, para. 29.

[113] *Industrial Relations: Programme for Action* (London, TUC, 1969).

CHAPTER 4

[1] See, for example, J. Hughes, *Trade Union Structure and Government*, Research Paper 5 (Part 1) of the Royal Commission on Trade Unions and Employers' Associations (London, HMSO, 1967), pp. 3–4. Other countries have different patterns, e.g. in Japan enterprise unions are found. See S. B. Levine, 'Unionization of White-Collar Employees in Japan', in A. Sturmthal (ed.), *White-Collar Trade Unions* (Urbana, Ill., University of Illinois Press, 1967), pp. 235–7.

[2] H. A. Turner, *Trade Union Growth, Structure and Policy* (London, Allen & Unwin, 1962).

[3] Hughes, op. cit., p. 17.

[4] *Report of the Royal Commission on Trade Unions and Employers' Associations 1965–8*, Cmnd. 3623 (London, HMSO, 1968), p. 181.

[5] D. Lockwood, *The Blackcoated Worker* (London, Allen & Unwin, 1958), pp. 195–8.

[6] *Minutes of Evidence of the Association of Supervisory Staffs,*

Executives and Technicians (ASSET) to the Royal Commission on Trade Unions and Employers' Associations (London, HMSO, 1967), pp. 2242 and 2269.

[7] For the example of DATA see *Minutes of Evidence of the Draughtsmen's and Allied Technicians' Association (DATA) to the Royal Commission on Trade Unions and Employers' Associations* (London, HMSO, 1967), p. 1518.

[8] D. Volker, 'NALGO's Affiliation to the TUC', *BJIR*, March 1966, p. 74.

[9] Hughes, op. cit., pp. 24–5.

[10] Ibid., pp. 25–6.

[11] *Report of the Royal Commission . . .*, pp. 182–3.

[12] Ibid., pp. 185–6.

[13] Ibid., pp. 40–8.

[14] *In Place of Strife: A Policy for Industrial Relations*, Cmnd. 3888 (London, HMSO, 1969), pp. 14–15.

[15] Industrial Relations Bill, Bill 164 (London, HMSO, 1970), ss. 64–9.

[16] Industrial Relations Act 1971, ss. 44–5.

[17] Ibid., s. 54.

[18] Ibid., ss. 116–17.

[19] *Trade Union Congress Structure and Development* (London, TUC, 1970).

[20] A description of the internal organization of SOGAT is given in G. S. Bain, *The Growth of White-Collar Unionism* (London, Oxford University Press, 1970), pp. 103–5. NATSOPA has now broken away from SOGAT.

[21] *Union Reorganization* (Esher, GMWU, 1969), p. 4, para. 6.

[22] Bain, op. cit., pp. 111–12.

[23] *Minutes of Evidence of ASSET . . .*, pp. 2288–9.

[24] W. Roy, 'Membership Participation in the National Union of Teachers', *BJIR*, July 1964, pp. 191–4.

[25] Bain, op. cit., pp. 106–7.

[26] Ibid., p. 103.

[27] Roy, op. cit., p. 194.

[28] Turner, op. cit., p. 289ff.

[29] See J. Hughes, *Trade Union Structure and Government*, Research Paper 5 (Part 2) of the Royal Commission on Trade Unions and Employers' Associations (London, HMSO, 1968), pp. 17–20.

[30] Ibid., pp. 42–3.

[31] Ibid., pp. 45–6.

[32] Roy, op. cit., pp. 191–4.
[33] Hughes (Part 2), op. cit., pp. 5–7.
[34] *Minutes of Evidence of DATA* . . ., p. 1521.
[35] For the proposed principles of conduct of unions, see Industrial Relations Act 1971, s. 65.
[36] Ibid., ss. 34–6.
[37] Ibid., ss. 101, 116–17.
[38] *Report of the Royal Commission* . . ., p. 188; figures are for 1966.
[39] See H. A. Clegg, A. J. Killick and R. Adams, *Trade Union Officers* (Oxford, Blackwell, 1961), p. 50, Table 12.
[40] V. L. Allen, *Power in Trade Unions* (London, Longmans, 1954), p. 69.
[41] *Minutes of Evidence of ASSET* . . ., pp. 2244–5, para. 48.
[42] Hughes (Part 2), op. cit., pp. 42–3.
[43] Ibid., and Allen, op. cit., pp. 74–101.
[44] Clegg, Killick and Adams, op. cit., p. 47, Table 10.
[45] Ibid., p. 90.
[46] One example is in ASTMS. See *Minutes of Evidence of ASSET* . . ., p. 2288, paras 8537–9.
[47] Hughes (Part 2), op. cit., p. 41.
[48] *Report of the Chief Registrar of Friendly Societies for the Year 1970, Part 4, Trade Unions* (London, HMSO, 1971).
[49] See, for example, Lockwood, op. cit., p. 156ff.; and K. Prandy, *Professional Employees* (London, Faber & Faber, 1965), p. 137.
[50] *Report of the Royal Commission* . . ., pp. 211–12.
[51] *Written Evidence of NALGO to the Royal Commission on Trade Unions and Employers' Associations* (London, NALGO, 1965), p. 32.
[52] *Report of the Royal Commission* . . ., p. 209.
[53] Ibid., pp. 207, 214–15.
[54] Industrial Relations Act 1971, s. 63.
[55] Ibid., ss. 67–8.
[56] Ibid., ss. 78–9.
[57] Ibid., ss. 65–6.
[58] Ibid., ss. 81–3 and 87–91.
[59] Ibid., s. 96.
[60] Ibid., ss. 101, 117 and 132.
[61] Ibid., s. 5.
[62] Ibid., s. 45.
[63] Ibid., s. 11.
[64] Ibid., s. 17.

[65] Ibid., ss. 37 and 102.
[66] Lockwood, op. cit., p. 156ff.; and B. McCormick, 'Managerial Unionism in the Coal Industry', *British Journal of Sociology*, Vol. 11, 1960, p. 368.
[67] Volker, op. cit., p. 68.
[68] Bain, op. cit., p. 114.
[69] Volker, op. cit., pp. 63–70.
[70] *ABC of the TUC* (London, TUC, 1969), pp. 11–12, 23–4.
[71] See, for example, *Non-Manual Workers: Conference Report 1969* (London, TUC, 1969).
[72] *Industrial Relations: Programme for Action* (London, TUC, 1969), pp. 96–7.
[73] *Report of the Chief Registrar . . .*, p. 15.
[74] *Report of the Chief Registrar of Friendly Societies for the Year 1969, Part 4, Trade Unions* (London, HMSO, 1970), pp. 16–17.
[75] M. Harrison, *Trade Unions and the Labour Party since 1945* (London, Allen & Unwin, 1960), pp. 61–6.
[76] Ibid., pp. 325–6.
[77] See S. B. Levine, 'The White-Collar, Blue-Collar Alliance in Japan', Symposium, *Industrial Relations*, October 1965, p. 114.
[78] Bain, op. cit., pp. 118–19.
[79] See Prandy, op. cit., Chapter 8.
[80] Lockwood, op. cit., p. 160; figure is for 1951.
[81] *Minutes of Evidence of DATA . . .*, p. 1535. Figure is for 1966.
[82] W. Pickles, 'Trade Unions in the Political Climate', in B. C. Roberts (ed.), *Industrial Relations – Contemporary Problems and Perspectives* (London, Methuen, 1968), p. 276. Figure is for 1964.
[83] V. L. Allen, *Trade Unions and the Government* (London, Longmans, 1960), p. 311.
[84] See *In Place of Strife . . .*, and Industrial Relations Bill.
[85] *Minutes of Evidence of the National Federation of Professional Workers (NFPW) to the Royal Commission on Trade Unions and Employers' Associations* (London, HMSO, 1966), p. 1055. Figures are for 1966.
[86] Volker, op. cit. ,pp. 60–5; and S. Lerner, 'The Organization and Structure of Trade Unions', in Roberts (ed.), op. cit., p. 68.
[87] See Sturmthal (ed.), op. cit., p. 383.
[88] A. Fox, *Industrial Sociology and Industrial Relations*, Research Paper 3 of the Royal Commission on Trade Unions and Employers' Associations (London, HMSO, 1966), p. 7.
[89] See A. Flanders, 'Collective Bargaining: A Theoretical

Analysis', *BJIR*, March 1968, p. 26; Hughes (Part 1), op. cit., p. 42; *Minutes of Evidence of NFPW* . . ., p. 1057.

[90] See, for example, A. Flanders, *Trade Unions* (London, Hutchinson, 1968), pp. 133–45.

[91] V. Burke, *Teachers in Turmoil* (Harmondsworth, Penguin, 1971), pp. 114–18. For a full discussion of the part played by politics in education see R. A. Manzer, *Teachers and Politics* (Manchester, Manchester University Press, 1970).

[92] Clegg, Killick and Adams, op. cit., p. 185.

[93] H. M. Douty, 'Salary Determination for White-Collar Civil Servants in Great Britain', *Monthly Labour Review*, November 1960, p. 1161.

[94] *Industrial Relations Handbook* (London, HMSO, 1961), pp. 98–103.

[95] For notes on formal joint negotiating machinery in both public and private sectors, see ibid., Chapters III, IV and V.

[96] Volker, op. cit., p. 71.

[97] R. M. Blackburn, *Union Character and Social Class* (London, Batsford, 1967), pp. 90–1.

[98] *Minutes of Evidence of DATA* . . ., p. 1528, para. 76.

[99] R. K. Kelsall and H. M. Kelsall, *The School Teacher in England and the United States: The Findings of Empirical Research* (London, Pergamon, 1969), pp. 143–59. The position is broadly similar in the United States.

[100] Burke, op. cit., p. 157.

[101] Roy, op. cit., pp. 195–206.

[102] Burke, op. cit., pp. 21 and 28–40.

[103] For a full report of the campaign, see ibid., Part II.

[104] See, for example, *The Guardian*, 6 October 1969.

[105] Lockwood, op. cit., pp. 193–4; and *Minutes of Evidence of ASSET* . . ., p. 2244.

[106] Industrial Relations Act 1971, ss. 37–43.

[107] Ibid., ss. 34–6.

[108] *Minutes of Evidence of DATA* . . ., p. 1529; and *Minutes of Evidence of NFPW* . . ., p. 1064.

[109] Industrial Relations Act 1971, ss. 7, 11–16, 17–18.

[110] Ibid., Schedule 1, s. 5.

[111] Ibid., ss. 56 and 102.

[112] Ibid., ss. 96 and 147.

[113] *In Place of Strife* . . ., pp. 16–17; *Report of the Royal Commission* . . ., p. 257; and *Minutes of Evidence of ASSET* . . ., pp. 2273–4.

[114] *Written Evidence of NALGO . . .*, p. 12; and *Report of the Royal Commission . . .*, pp. 258–9.

[115] *You and the ATTI* (London, ATTI, August 1969).

[116] Quoted in Blackburn, op. cit., p. 82. See also the example of ASTMS in Prandy, op. cit., p. 138; and *The Case for the British Manager* (London, ASTMS, 1969), p. 48.

[117] Kelsall and Kelsall, op. cit., pp. 143–4.

[118] *Teacher Education and Training* (London, HMSO, 1972).

[119] Burke, op. cit., pp. 150–5; and Kelsall and Kelsall, op. cit., pp. 154–6.

[120] Burke, op. cit., p. 144.

[121] *Minutes of Evidence of DATA . . .*, pp. 1519–21.

[122] G. S. Bain, *Trade Union Growth and Recognition*, Research Paper 6 of the Royal Commission on Trade Unions and Employers' Associations (London, HMSO, 1967), p. 93.

[123] See Fox, op. cit., pp. 3–4.

[124] Bain (1967), op. cit., p. 93.

[125] O. Robinson, 'Representation of the White-Collar Worker: The Bank Staff Associations in Britain', *BJIR*, March 1969, p. 23.

[126] Blackburn, op. cit., pp. 142–68.

[127] *Minutes of Evidence of NFPW . . .*, pp. 1069–70.

[128] *Report of the Inquiry by the Honourable Lord Cameron, DSC, QC, into the complaint made by the National Union of Bank Employees on 12th March 1962, to the Committee on Freedom of Association of the International Labour Organization* (London, HMSO, 1963).

[129] Robinson, op. cit., pp. 27–34, 38–40.

[130] Blackburn, op. cit., pp. 142ff. and 251.

[131] Ibid., p. 174.

[132] Robinson, op. cit., pp. 21–2.

[133] A. M. Carr-Saunders and P. A. Wilson, *The Professions*, (London, Frank Cass, 1964), pp. 328–30.

[134] Prandy, op. cit., pp. 76–8.

[135] K. Prandy, 'Professional Organizations in Great Britain', Symposium, *Industrial Relations*, October 1965, p. 75.

[136] Industrial Relations Act 1971, ss. 84–6.

[137] Professional unions in the United States act in a similar way. See B. Goldstein, 'Some Aspects of the Nature of Unionism among Salaried Professionals in Industry', *American Sociological Review*, Vol. 20, 1955, p. 204.

[138] Roberts, op. cit., p. 13.

[139] See, for example, H. Eckstein, *Pressure Group Politics* (London, Allen & Unwin, 1960), pp. 49–51.

[140] Ibid., pp. 58–60.

[141] Ibid., pp. 62–4.

[142] *Industrial Relations Handbook*, pp. 99–102.

[143] See, for example, G. Routh, 'White-Collar Unions in the United Kingdom', in A. Sturmthal (ed.), op. cit., p. 175; and Eckstein, op. cit., pp. 40–1.

[144] Quoted in *The Guardian*, 29 June 1970.

[145] *Engineers' Guild: An Introduction to its Aims and Achievements*, 1959; cited in Prandy, *Professional Employees* . . ., p. 75.

[146] Ibid., p. 80 and Chapter 6.

[147] Ibid., pp. 80–1.

[148] See, for example, *The Sunday Times*, 16 August 1970.

[149] *Memorandum of Association*, Institution of Metallurgists, 1954, p. 3; cited in Prandy, *Professional Employees* . . ., p. 73.

[150] Ibid., p. 78.

[151] Prandy, *Professional Organizations* . . ., p. 74.

Index